COMPLETE
HOME
CRAFTS

MIRANDA INNES.

COMPLETE HOME CRAFTS

Photography by Clive Streeter

DK PUBLISHING, INC.

For Roger, without whose dedication and generosity
this book would not exist

A DK PUBLISHING BOOK

Conceived, edited, and designed
by Collins & Brown Limited

Project Editor: Heather Dewhurst
Editorial Director: Colin Ziegler
Assistant Editor: Claire Waite

Art Director: Roger Bristow
Art Editor: Steve Wooster
Designer: Claire Graham
For pages 170-216, Marnie Searchwell
and Alison Verity

Photography: Clive Streeter
For pages 170-216, Sam Lloyd
For pages 138-139, Julie Fisher
For pages 92-95, 130-131, 158-159,
162-163, Steve Gorton
Stylist: Leanne Mackenzie

First American Edition, 1997
2 4 6 8 10 9 7 5 3 1

Published in the United States by
DK Publishing, Inc., 95 Madison Avenue
New York, New York 10016
Visit us on the World Wide Web at http://www.dk.com

Copyright © 1997 Dorling Kindersley Limited, London
Text copyright © 1997 Miranda Innes

Innes, Miranda.
    Complete home crafts / by Miranda Innes.
        p.   cm.
    Includes index.
    ISBN 0-7894-1972-6
    1. Handicraft. 2. House furnishings. 3. Interior decoration.
I. Title.
TT157.I5597 1997   97-16402
745.5–dc21   CIP

Printed and bound in Great Britain
by Butler and Tanner Ltd

CONTENTS

INTRODUCTION

GOLDFINCHES ARE KNOWN to decorate their nests with a spray of forget-me-nots and a fern frond or two in the interests of promoting a happy home life. If they feel moved to such efforts, there is every reason why humans should enjoy the pleasures of adding a touch of paint or a waft of fabric to their homes. Decorating is one of life's most innocent and cheering pastimes; there is little to compare with the heady excitement of turning a junk-shop discovery into an heirloom, or a bundle of sale remnants into a sumptuous cushion. This is how good, warm feelings begin, and how a house magically transmutes into a home.

To begin with, you may feel daunted by the whole creative process, and have at the back of your mind the notion that you should have had art school training, or that you should be an expert to wield brush or sewing machine. This book is intended to be a confidence booster, to demonstrate that you do not have to be an interior designer to make your home look stunning. Absolute perfection is not the object of crafts – a machine can turn out perfect clones – but the point of making something yourself is that it is endowed with your character and quirks. In an age of machine manufacturing, signs of originality and personality are precious, and whatever you choose to make, the way you do it will be as unique as your signature.

GETTING ORGANIZED

This book is divided into rooms, and each is a given general color theme. This is an instant way of taming color chaos that can descend on homes and unsettle people. It is also a way of helping to decide what color to paint a frame or what fabric to use to make a cushion. Feel free to follow these color choices, or to substitute your own preferences.

Once you have settled on a color scheme to follow, but before you begin to make anything, look afresh at your existing

possessions. You could recycle the things you can't bear to part with – throw out the chipped, broken, and tattered with a great sigh of relief, and make the most of those things that give enduring pleasure. Take your ragbag, for instance. If you have the tiniest iota of the sentimental old fool in you, you will have bits and pieces dating back decades. If you can get the different fabrics and colors to coordinate, the answer may be to combine them in pieced and appliquéd cushion covers. Men's old pinstriped cotton shirts make extremely stylish patchwork quilts, and brushed cotton checks in related colors can be pieced in simple squares and knotted to a cotton interlining to make deliciously cozy winter curtains.

If you have amassed lots of clutter and would like either to hide it or alternatively to show it off, try building or painting shelves or frames in which to flatter it, or boxes in which to conceal it. Displaying collections of favorite objects is best served by editing them down first to those that look good together. There are plenty of examples shown in the book, and, once you start, you will come up with ideas of your own.

LOOKING FOR INSPIRATION

One of the great pleasures of making things for your home is starting from scratch, buying pristine whitewood blanks and carefully chosen paints, or delicious lengths of shot silk, with a specific object and purpose in mind. This is where searching through magazines for great color partnerships or motifs to steal comes into its own. The vibrant Persian table rug in a Holbein painting may provide inspiration for shades and tones that you might use on your own tablecloth. Mogul miniatures

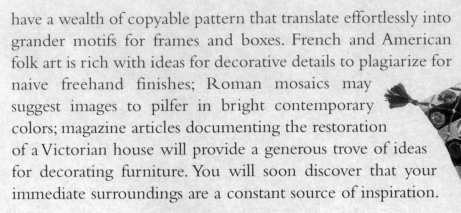

have a wealth of copyable pattern that translate effortlessly into grander motifs for frames and boxes. French and American folk art is rich with ideas for decorative details to plagiarize for naive freehand finishes; Roman mosaics may suggest images to pilfer in bright contemporary colors; magazine articles documenting the restoration of a Victorian house will provide a generous trove of ideas for decorating furniture. You will soon discover that your immediate surroundings are a constant source of inspiration.

ENJOYING YOURSELF

Making things for your home is quite simply thrilling. Mastering any of the manageable skills required to paint a box or stitch a cushion requires total concentration, and the complete absorption of creating something from scratch will make time fly. And for no very particular reason, it will also make your troubles diminish. Professional craftspeople have their moments of anxiety when the rent is due, but as a tribe they exude the quiet confidence of people who have discovered the secret of life. Whatever mysterious human need is satisfied by making things, the effect is cumulative – the more you do, the more you *can* do.

TOOLS AND MATERIALS

None of the projects in this book requires wildly expensive or esoteric equipment; most of the tools and materials can be bought locally or by mail order. It is, however, a sad fact that poor-quality tools cause more trouble than you save. Buy as good as you can afford, and feel the quality and springiness of the bristles in the case of a brush, or the weight and balance of the handle in the case of a craft knife. For découpage you will need blades, scissors, and a cutting mat. Patchwork makers use a cutting mat and a rotary cutter to produce piles of

identically shaped pieces of fabric. A craft knife is necessary for cutting stencils, unless you can track down one of the excellent heated stencil cutters that glide smoothly through acetate and enable you to cut out intricate shapes.

Most paints in this book are either acrylic or latex, which are easy to use, quick drying, nontoxic, water soluble, and adaptable. A fascinating range of crackle finishes, varnishes of various kinds, and scumble glazes that all work with acrylic paints is also available.

GETTING STARTED

In an ideal world you would have a studio dedicated to your creative efforts. The sad fact is that most of us have to work on the kitchen table, interrupted by an uncomprehending family demanding food. Fortunately, most of the projects in this book can be made quickly, and if you can evict the children for the best part of a single day, there is a good chance you will have finished by the time they return to mess with the glue and knock over your paint. However, ruthless organization does pay dividends. It makes sense to clear as big a space as possible, and to wipe down and cover your work surfaces with newspaper or plastic.

It has become something of a cliché that a perfect finish is not the goal, but it remains true. Among the many reasons to make things yourself, one of the most compelling is the fact that your work will be uniquely yours. You can make whatever you like exactly as you want it. So, if the urge seizes you, start today. You probably already have half the materials on hand, and just need a nudge to assemble something terrific. Clear a large work area, lay out all your bits and pieces, ponder colors, textures, and finishes, turn on the radio, and dig in. Making something is such a pleasure in itself, it is a glorious bonus if you end up with something usable and attractive.

Entrances & Exits

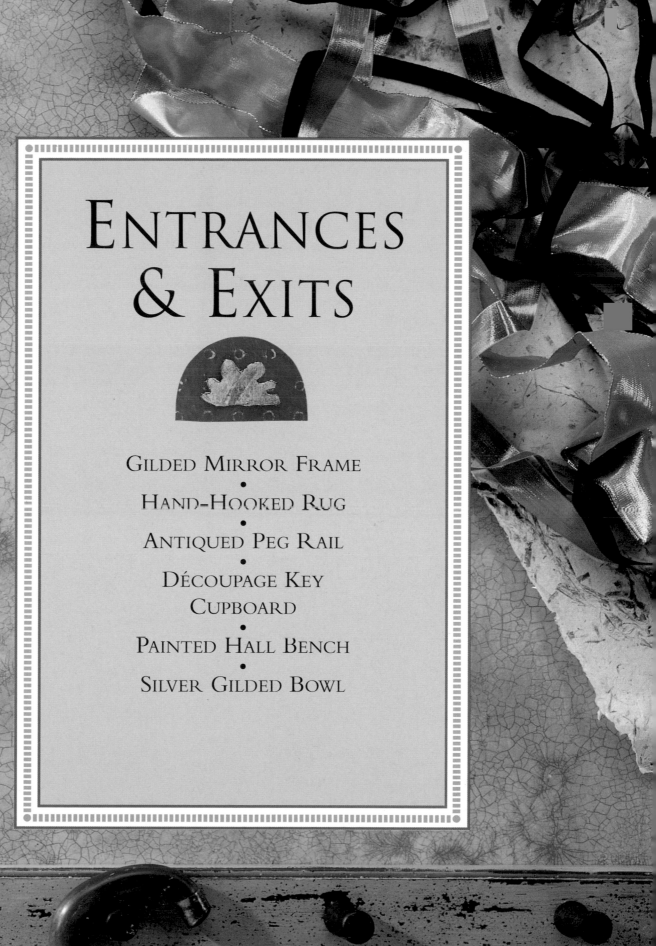

GILDED MIRROR FRAME

MATERIALS

- Mirror frame and mirror
- Mounting board
- Bronze powder
- PVA glue
- Water
- Gold powder
- Gold wrapping paper
- Gold transfer paper

THIS FRAME is a glittering example of making little into plenty – the materials are cheap and easy to come by, and the effect is of positively Byzantine richness, combined with a hint of Mayan mystery. This mirror also has the extra advantage of framing faces in something glamorous – offering your guests a warm welcome or gracious exit. It is simple to make and requires just a modicum of skill in the shaping and cutting. The decoration needs only a steady hand and a dash of panache.

Gilt Options

Rich, tawny shades of bronze and a splash of pink speckled with different kinds of gold make this humble frame luxurious. Blue, purple, ruby, and silver would have a grand and opulent effect.

MAKING THE FRAME

1 Designing the frame
Draw the shape of your mirror frame on mounting board. Center a semicircle on the top edge of the frame. Carefully cut out the penciled shape using a craft or utility knife. Be sure to protect your work surface with a cutting mat or a piece of cardboard.

2 Painting the frame
Using PVA glue, attach the mounting board shape to the frame. Mix bronze powder with a little PVA glue and water until it is the consistency of cream. Paint this on to the semicircular area of the mounting board. With a mix of gold powder, PVA glue, and water, paint the rest of the board. Leave to dry.

DECORATING THE FRAME

2 Enriching the collage
Embellish the decoration further by gluing small squares of wrapping paper and gold transfer paper around the edge of the frame. For a matte effect, leave the backing paper in place on some of the squares of gold transfer paper. Leave to dry.

1 Gluing on gold strips
Tear or cut gold wrapping paper into small strips about 1 in (2.5 cm) long and ¼ in (6 mm) wide. Paint each strip individually with PVA glue and stick them around the inner edge of the frame. Repeat to decorate the outer edges of the frame.

3 Scoring the frame
Using the back of a craft knife blade, make decorative scratches, squiggles, and scored lines on the frame. Insert the mirror in the frame and hang it in a place of honor on the wall.

HAND-HOOKED RUG

MATERIALS
- Burlap
- Rug frame (optional)
- Strong thread
- Assorted fabric strips,
  ⅝ in (1.5 cm) wide

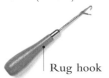

Rug hook

RAG RUGS HAVE A LONG and honorable history, and are a splendidly thrifty way to recycle your old T-shirts, those wild-colored tights that you instantly regretted buying, and your beloved but tired old socks. Choose colors that look good in a heap, and avoid creating large areas of unrelieved single colors. The charm of handmade things lies in their individuality and liveliness, and vividly contrasting speckles are an effortless way to achieve this. Using a frame makes the work easier, but is not essential.

PREPARING THE BURLAP

1 Marking out the design
Draw the design for your rug on burlap with a marker. Choose simple shapes and patterns. This design is of hearts, curlicues, and flowers.

2 Stretching the burlap
Attach the burlap to a rug frame by stitching two opposite ends to the webbing on the bar of the frame with strong thread. Wind the burlap around the bar of the frame until only about 18 in (45 cm) of the burlap is visible. This will stretch it and hold it tight.

A Hearty Welcome
Hearts and flowers may be familiar design motifs, but they can hardly be bettered for their welcome message (right). These are so lively and whimsical that they promise an entertaining sojourn for one's guests.

HOOKING THE RUG

1 Making fabric loops
Hold a fabric strip beneath the burlap and push the hook through the burlap from above. Guide the fabric over the hook to make a loop. Pull the hook up through the burlap, bringing up the end of the strip. Push the hook down the next hole in the burlap, guide the fabric onto the hook (see inset), and pull through the burlap to form a loop ⅝ in (1.5 cm) high on the surface.

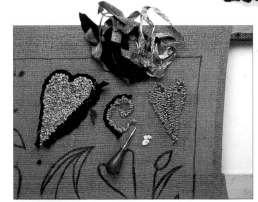

2 Filling in motifs
Continue to form loops to fill in each motif. When you reach the end of a fabric strip, pull the end to the top side and trim off to the level of the loops. Change fabric colors when desired.

3 **Hooking background**
When you have filled in the pattern motifs, continue forming loops to fill in the background of the design. Here, the heart and flower motifs stand out against a predominantly black background.

4 **Hemming the rug**
When the design is completed, remove the burlap from the frame and press the back. Then turn the edges under and hem with strong thread. Press again.

ANTIQUED PEG RAIL

MATERIALS

- Wooden peg rail and pegs
- Water-based paint: black, yellow
- Shellac sanding sealer
- Sand
- Wood stain
- Wood glue
- Clear furniture wax

A BRISK AIR OF Shaker utility and purpose characterizes this rustic peg rail, and there is a breezy simplicity about its construction. Using sand to craze the paint finish is unusual but easy, and results in a convincing look of weathered old age, a look that is emphasized by burnishing the paint off altogether on the edge of the rail, as if through decades of use. Clear wax brings out the country colors of creosote and wheat to make the perfect resting place for your bucolic straw bonnet.

The Shakers used pegs to hang up just about everything, from clothes and hats to chairs and cabinets, and the idea can be adapted to suit today's lifestyle – you will always find uses for pegs, so the longer you make the rail, the better it will be.

All-Purpose Pegs

Peg rails (below) are useful anywhere in the home – for towels in the bathroom, bathrobes in the bedroom, dish towels and other hangable paraphernalia in the kitchen, and for hats, bags, dog leashes, coats, and scarves in the hall. Just make them twice as long as you think you'll need, and you'll get it about right.

PAINTING THE RAIL

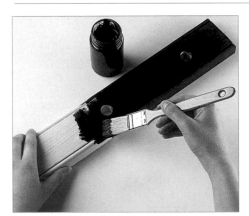

1 Painting the base coat
Paint the front and the sides of the peg rail with a coat of black water-based paint, and allow to dry.

2 Sprinkling on sand
Apply a coat of shellac sanding sealer over the peg rail. Before it dries, sprinkle sand all over the wet surface. Let dry.

3 Painting the top coat
Brush a coat of yellow water-based paint over the sandy surface of the peg rail, applying it thickly to avoid dislodging the grains of sand. Allow to dry.

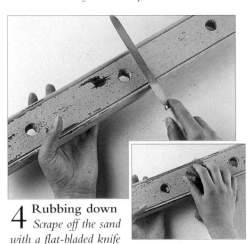

4 Rubbing down
Scrape off the sand with a flat-bladed knife to reveal patches of the base coat. Rub the surface down more with steel wool (see inset).

16

PAINTING AND ATTACHING THE PEGS

1 Applying wood stain
Paint the pegs with a coat of wood stain and allow to dry. You need only paint the part of the peg that will be visible when it is hammered into the rail.

2 Attaching the pegs
Apply wood glue onto the sides of the peg holes from the back of the peg rail. Hammer a peg into each hole, holding a small block of wood between the hammer and the peg to avoid denting the peg.

3 Waxing the peg rail
Using a soft cloth, rub clear furniture wax over the peg rail to seal the surface. Drill a hole at each end of the rail and attach it to the wall with screws.

DÉCOUPAGE KEY CUPBOARD

MATERIALS

- Wooden key cabinet
- Latex paint: white, black
- White paper
- Black-and-white key illustrations
- PVA glue

KEYS HAVE A WAY OF disappearing right when you need them, so the well-organized household has a key cabinet, and the very well-organized household labels the keys. Then you don't have to try every single key each time you want to padlock the tool box or get into the cellar. You can do no better than highlighting the purpose of your cabinet with crisp engravings photocopied from a Victorian-style catalog or another source. Keys and padlocks can make very attractive graphic images. To keep them looking good, it would be wise to seal the finished cabinet with water-based varnish. Small things like this little cabinet are fun and quick to do, and you can experiment endlessly on a theme of keys, using stamps cut from linoleum, erasers, or humble spuds.

PREPARING THE CUPBOARD AND DÉCOUPAGE

1 Painting the cabinet
Paint the key cabinet all over, both inside and out, with a coat of white latex paint. Let dry.

2 Cutting out key images
Measure the recess on the cabinet front. Cut out a piece of white paper to the same measurements. Cut out images of black-and-white engravings or photocopies of keys, and stick them down on the paper panel using white glue.

ADDING THE DECORATION

1 Gluing on paper panel
Using PVA glue, stick plain white paper onto the cabinet. Then apply PVA glue to the back of the decorated paper panel and attach this to the front of the cupboard. Be sure that the paper is straight, and smooth it in place to remove any air bubbles.

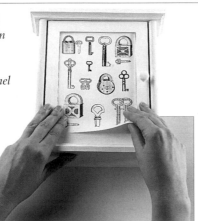

2 Decorating the sides
Repeat to decorate the sides, top, and bottom of the key cabinet with similarly decorated paper panels. Paint the cupboard knob with black latex paint and let dry.

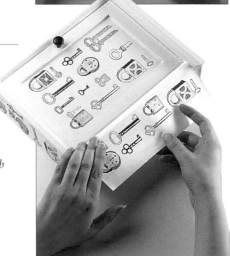

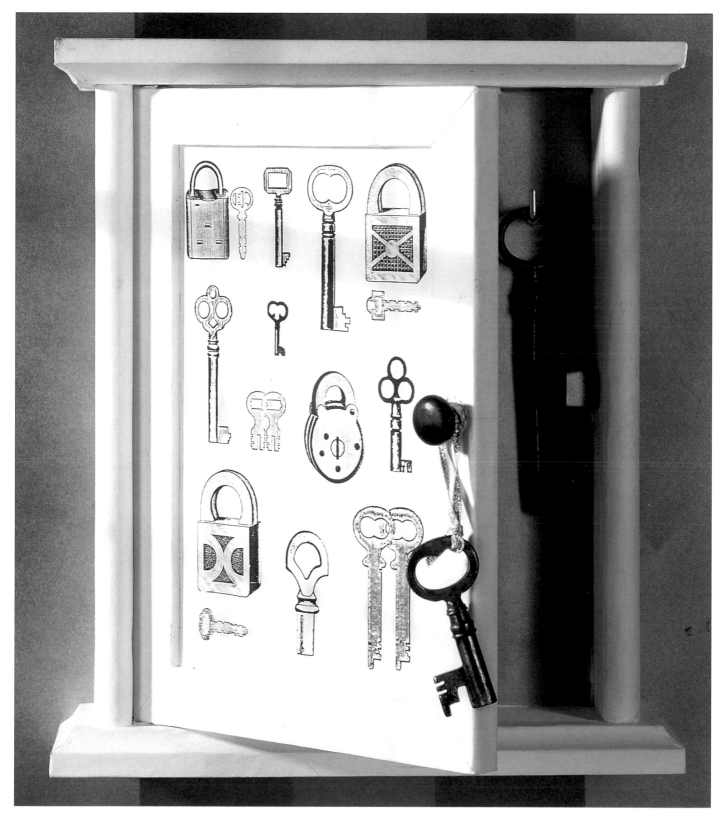

Key Feature

From the moment you are given your first bicycle and have to padlock it, life is marked by the acquisition of a growing number of keys. Hope springs eternal that if only, like the Shakers, one had a place for everything and everything in its place, one would not need to fritter away so many precious hours hunting. This cabinet (above) might just hold the key to less frantic departures.

DECORATIVE EXTRAS

A CLEAR GRAPHIC IMAGE, such as keys in all their multifarious variations, is open to all kinds of possibilities. Here we show real and engraved keys in different permutations – photocopied and colored, rubbed using a crayon, and transferred to different-colored papers. Keys have a strong symbolic significance, implying openings, possibilities, discoveries, the unknown, mysteries solved, as well as the more familiar connotation of coming of age. There are plenty of other simple symbols that can be exploited in this way – hearts, moon and stars, doves, fleurs-de-lis. They are all part of our mythology and countless representations exist, from the bold images of heraldry and Japanese family crests down to wrapping paper, from which to take inspiration. For a key cupboard, keys are obviously apposite and useful. Other experiments could be pursued using photographs, employing the enlarging or reducing facilities of photocopiers, photocopying actual keys in black and white, or against a colored background in color, and using rubber stamps in formal or random patterns.

Misty Silhouettes

The Victorians used this technique to show off all sorts of things with intricate outlines, such as fern fronds, shells, and feathers. They would use these to build up patterns, spraying in black or dark brown to achieve a lustrous finish akin to lacquer. In the age before aerosol paint, this had to be done by blowing the paint with a diffuser, an unpredictable business that required experience and practice to achieve a fine mist of color. Fortunately, we can now call on spray paint in a wealth of colors, and use spray mount to hold complicated or delicate objects in position. Keys are heavy enough to behave themselves. These four variations on the theme of keys as stencils could be put together in a jigsaw of brown and gold. You could liven up the background by spraying through a paper doily.

• *Assemble a collection of interestingly shaped keys and arrange them on plain or colored paper. Then simply spray a fine mist of aerosol paint over the keys. To add interest to the motifs, spatter your finished design using a painty toothbrush and a piece of cardboard.*

Color Keys

This trio of keys is photocopied and colored to antiquity with tea. This is easily done with a strong brew, but coffee or dilute burnt umber watercolor paint would work just as well.

• *To give an aged look to paper, simply pour hot water into a mug, add a tea bag, and allow to cool. Then brush the cold tea over the paper and let dry. For a wrinkle-free look, keep the wet paper stretched while drying by sticking it to a work surface with brown packing tape.*

Child's Play

Everyone must have whiled away ten minutes as a child by doing rubbings of coins, and then been amazed as a crisp profile of a presidential dignitary appeared on the paper as if by magic. The magic tended to be short-lived due to the paucity of small, flat, intricately textured objects to reproduce. Keys are a glorious discovery, since they have all the necessary attributes, being small and sharply defined, and usually with interesting surface detail. These are the ones to look for – a nicely toothed and ribbed front door key is perfect.

• *Place the key on a flat surface and lay your paper on top. Holding the paper and key carefully to ensure that they do not slip, gently rub a crayon over the paper until the impression of the key is revealed. Using smooth, thin paper, and applying an even pressure with a fine quality crayon gives the most detail. Textured paper and the side of a wax crayon give a more impressionistic or ghostlike look.*

Golden Possibilities

A richly burnished look comes from using combinations of gold spray paint and gold Dutch metal leaf. Use keys as stencils, and spray gold paint over the top. Alternatively, cut a potato print of a key and print onto Dutch metal leaf.

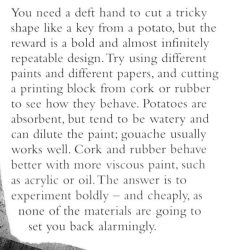

You need a deft hand to cut a tricky shape like a key from a potato, but the reward is a bold and almost infinitely repeatable design. Try using different paints and different papers, and cutting a printing block from cork or rubber to see how they behave. Potatoes are absorbent, but tend to be watery and can dilute the paint; gouache usually works well. Cork and rubber behave better with more viscous paint, such as acrylic or oil. The answer is to experiment boldly – and cheaply, as none of the materials are going to set you back alarmingly.

• *To make a potato print, cut a potato in half and blot the cut surface with a paper towel. Hold a key on the surface and carefully make an incision around the outline with a sharp craft knife. Remove the key, then cut away the potato so that the key image stands high.*

Paper Patchwork

The paneled door of this little key cupboard is like a picture frame, with textured handmade paper setting off a collage of different colors and methods. This requires nothing more than a sharp craft knife, PVA glue, and a certain panache. A small object like this is an ideal place to discover the pleasure of playing with images on paper.

• *Decorate a few pieces of paper with different key images. Cut them into squares using a sharp craft knife. Then glue the paper squares onto the background paper using PVA glue. Finally, apply a coat of varnish to seal.*

PAINTED HALL BENCH

MATERIALS
- Wooden bench
- Black wood stain
- Water
- Gold metallic paint
- Latex paint: red, cream
- Decorative motif
- Acrylic varnish

THIS UNPRETENTIOUS BOX bench, into which you can throw galoshes, footballs, and old dog blankets, has been made to look like a rajah's throne through the simple application of paint and an evening's work. There is no need to decorate the bench more, but if you do have a passion for pattern, a glance through a stack of art and antique books will give you ideas for simple repeating patterns with which to deck the open areas. These decorating techniques would give an equally exciting look to any piece of wooden furniture.

Benchmarks
The designs applied to this seat were copied from the border pattern on a painted mirror frame from India. The most difficult aspect was achieving straight border lines of red and gold.

STAINING AND PAINTING

1 Applying wood stain
Adding water and stirring thoroughly, dilute the black wood stain. Using a household painting brush, coat the wooden bench liberally, until the entire surface is covered. Let dry.

2 Lining the bench
Using an artist's brush and gold metallic paint, paint a fine gold line along all the edges of the bench. Then paint a fine red line inside each gold line using red latex paint (see inset).

3 Painting dots
When dry, add small dots of cream paint in between the painted lines for decoration. Try to keep an equal distance between each painted dot. Let dry.

4 Transferring a design
Transfer a decorative motif onto the backrest of the bench. To do this, place a piece of transfer paper over the backrest. Lay the traced motif on top and tape in position. Go over the outline with a pencil. Repeat along the entire back rest.

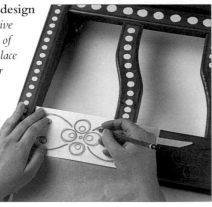

5 Painting the motifs
Using an artist's brush, carefully paint over the outlines of the motifs with gold metallic paint. Let dry. Add additional decorative motifs as required. Apply a coat of acrylic varnish to seal.

DECORATIVE EXTRAS

WOODEN CHESTS HAVE always been the perfect blank canvas upon which many creative homemakers have painted their favorite motifs, entwined initials, and simple repeating patterns. A straightforward, businesslike hall bench has the same potential, and is an indispensable piece of furniture, with its obliging capacity to hide hallway clutter and give you a convenient and comfortable perch from which to struggle with your galoshes. Your artistry may take a folksy tone, or you might take inspiration from Elizabethan coffers, Spanish stamped leather and brass trunks, or the wild geometry of Rajasthani quilt boxes. There are countless sources of design and color partnerships to be found in French and American traditional painted furniture, or you could shamelessly plagiarize motifs and patterns from works of high art. You can limit yourself to decorative borders and a roundel, or you can cover the whole thing with a bouquet of glorious color.

Aztec Sunburst

This simple but dramatic design, painted in strong hot colors, was created by stippling through a very straightforward stencil. The sunburst design – the part that is in yellow – was traced from a pattern book, enlarged, then transferred onto stencil cardboard and cut out. The colors could be varied to suit your individual decor, and simpler motifs could be substituted if desired.

● *First paint the background yellow and leave to dry. Place the cut stencil over the yellow background, securing it in place with masking tape. Then, using a stencil brush, lightly brush black around the outside of the stencil, then stipple cinnabar-colored paint through the holes in the stencil. For the best results, use very little paint on the brush.*

Massachusetts Meadow

This simple and effective motif was taken from an early 19th-century painted toleware coffee pot from Massachusetts. A little calculation and careful measurement with steel ruler and T-square is required to make sure that a repeating pattern is evenly spaced, but the flowers do not need to be identical. This trio of colors is particularly rich and warm.

● *First plan the roundel using a circle of paper. Fold it in four and sketch a flower in each quarter. Trace the flowers onto the wood with carbon paper. Plan the red wreath in the same way, marking off the edge of the four segments of folded paper into roughly equidistant quarters, and then sketching the red motifs in place by eye, having drawn a smaller circle to define the pattern's edge. Sketch the top border on paper, and then transfer it with carbon paper. Mark the placing of the flowers using a ruler, then paint them freehand. If you do happen to make a mistake, it is a simple matter to paint it out and start again.*

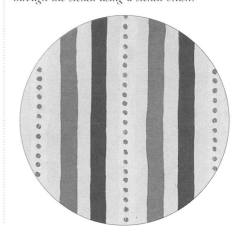

Cool Gustavian Stripes

Muted Swedish paint colors have been used here in a casual freehand design of stripes, enlivened by a row of stenciled dots. The soft blues and greens would be perfect for a country hallway, and the seat would happily hide walking boots and dog leashes, blending beautifully with terra-cotta floor tiles and blond wood.

• *Make a simple dot stencil by using a hole punch to punch regular, even-sized holes into stencil cardboard. Then position the stencil over the painted stripes when dry, and dab paint through the stencil using a stencil brush.*

Raj Remembered

This design was taken from a Rajput gouache depicting a ruler and his nobles. The actual pattern is made up of tiny elements from the painting – stripes taken from the royal cushions, and flowers from his embroidered carpet.

• *Painting stripes is a simple matter of measuring and drawing lines to follow freehand with paint. The hardest part is getting a "loose" straight edge, and you could use masking tape if you are a stickler for precision. Position the green drops by careful measuring, and place the flowers by eye.*

The stripes on the body of the bench need a little calculation in order to avoid odd half-stripes at the sides. But with an all-over design, the eye is very forgiving. Paint the drops with a fine artist's brush on diagonals measured and drawn lightly in pencil.

Antique Flowers

This curiously Tudor-looking design was taken from a crudely colored, 19th-century French religious woodcut showing St. Catherine and a bevy of angels. The borders were pillaged unchanged while the flowers came from the corners of the print. The colors have a cool, classic freshness. When copying from an original piece, it is worth paying attention to the details. This woodcut has a pleasantly rough quality in all its tiny lines and boxes, which is cheeringly easy to emulate.

them in with a slightly lighter tone. Paint the flowers carefully with a fine artist's brush. It pays to practice this a little on paper to become familiar with the optimum texture of paint and the fluency of line before painting the design on the bench.

• *The roundel is a series of concentric circles, drawn on paper, with the pattern sketched in place by eye. Absolute precision does not matter here. Draw the border and flowers roughly onto paper and then transfer them to the bench using carbon paper. To paint the design, first outline the blue leaves and lozenges in azure, and then fill*

SILVER GILDED BOWL

MATERIALS

- Plastic wrap
- Rabbit-skin glue
- Water
- Newsprint
- Rabbit-skin gesso
  (see pages 196–197)
- Bole: Blue, brown
- Tracing paper
- Low-tack tape
- Denatured alcohol
- Silver leaf
- Gilding finish
- Buffing compound

MOODY AND MAGNIFICENT, this bowl gives no indication of its humble newsprint origins. It is without question a work of art, and as such, you would not expect it to be the quick and easy work of a carefree moment – but some things in life are worth taking trouble over, and this is one of them. Papier-mâché, which is the basis, is a fine, fun, and usually somewhat unsophisticated medium, but here it has been refined with layers of gesso to give it weight, substance, and a surface as fine as porcelain. This is then given a rarefied finish with a fine clay, known as bole, and a magical flourish of silver leaf antiqued by a touch of simple alchemy.

The Best Circles

Duck à l'Orange was the inspiration for this darkly splendid bowl (right and below). Layers of gesso give a seductive solidity and elegant smoothness to the finish. The combination of polished bole and antiqued silver is about as grand as paper can become.

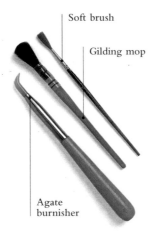

Soft brush

Gilding mop

Agate burnisher

Silver leaf

Gilder's tip

MAKING THE BOWL

1 Papering a bowl
Cover a mold with plastic wrap. Mix 1 part rabbit-skin glue to 10 parts water, soak for 30 minutes, then heat in a bain marie to dissolve the granules. Paste 12 layers of strips of newsprint over the wrap. Leave for 24 hours.

2 Applying gesso
Paint 6 layers of rabbit-skin gesso on the outside of the bowl. When dry, add 14 more layers, leaving each layer to go matte. Allow to dry for two days, remove it from the mold, and apply 10 layers to the inside in the same way.

3 Sanding the bowl
After the rough bowl has dried for a couple of days, sand the inside and outside of the bowl with very fine sandpaper to remove any unevenness. The bowl should now feel as smooth as porcelain.

PREPARING THE SURFACE

1 Applying bole
Using a soft brush, apply three coats of blue bole onto the outside of the bowl, brushing quickly. Then apply one or two coats of blue and brown bole mixed together, allowing some of the blue to show through. Finally, apply a coat of brown bole, allowing patches of the first two colors to show through. Let dry, then repeat the process on the inside.

> **PREPARING BOLE**
> *Mix 1 heaping teaspoon of each color of bole with a little slightly warmed rabbit-skin glue until the mixture is the thickness of cream. Strain through an old nylon stocking.*

2 Buffing with steel wool
When the bole has dried, take a pad of fine-grade steel wool and rub it over the outside and inside of the bowl to give the surface a soft sheen.

GILDING THE BOWL

1 Drawing the shapes
Cut out a duck and an orange from tracing paper and draw around them on the bowl using a pencil.

2 Edging with tape
Outline the edges of the drawn shapes on the bowl with pieces of low-tack tape to mask off the areas to be gilded.

3 Applying water and glue
Mix a cup of water with one drop each of rabbit-skin and denatured alcohol. Using a gilding mop, brush this over the shape to be gilded.

4 Applying silver leaf
Working quickly and using a gilder's tip, lay a piece of silver leaf carefully on the wet surface. Tap it into position with a soft brush. Repeat to cover all the area to be gilded, then leave to dry for 30 minutes.

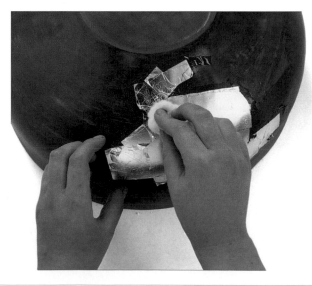

5 Rubbing down
Gently rub the surface of the silver leaf with a cotton ball to smooth it down and rub off any overlapping pieces. Carefully peel away the low-tack tape from around the edges to reveal the gilded shape. You can then repeat the process on other parts of the bowl, both outside and in.

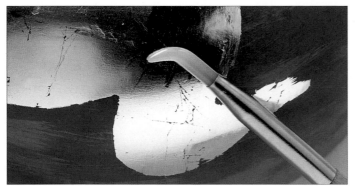

6 Burnishing the silver leaf
Burnish the gilded areas with an agate burnisher to press the silver leaf down securely on the surface, smooth out any creases, and bring out the shine.

7 Tarnishing the bowl
Dissolve 1 teaspoon of gilding finish in a cup of water. Brush this on the silver (right); it discolors in a few seconds. Leave to dry overnight. Seal the bowl with buffing compound, applied with a soft brush. Rub with fine-grade steel wool, then apply a final layer of compound.

DESIGN OPTIONS

Humps and Trunks

Simple, instantly recognizable shapes and subtle, dramatic colors are the distinctive and powerful features of this sophisticated gilding (below). The natural pigments can be layered so that the colors blend together in a lively finish.

Speckled Pear

This simple graphic image (left) was colored with three shades of green bole; the silver overlay was tarnished with bleach.

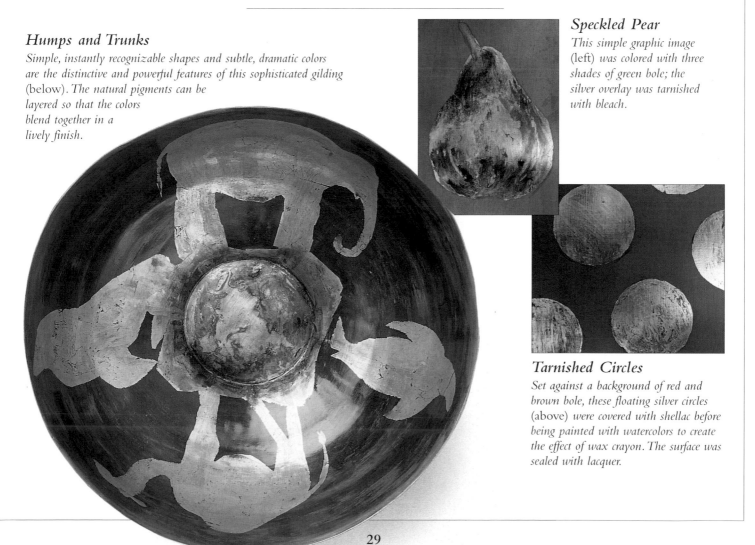

Tarnished Circles

Set against a background of red and brown bole, these floating silver circles (above) were covered with shellac before being painted with watercolors to create the effect of wax crayon. The surface was sealed with lacquer.

THE
LIVING
ROOM

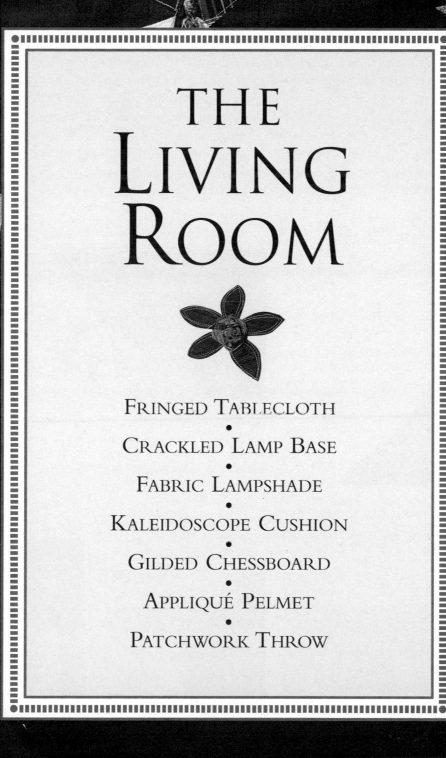

FRINGED TABLECLOTH

•

CRACKLED LAMP BASE

•

FABRIC LAMPSHADE

•

KALEIDOSCOPE CUSHION

•

GILDED CHESSBOARD

•

APPLIQUÉ PELMET

•

PATCHWORK THROW

FRINGED TABLECLOTH

MATERIALS

- Shot silk in two colors
- Remnants of colored silk, organza, and chiffon
- Fusible webbing
- Multicolored rayon thread
- Polyester lining fabric
- Sewing thread
- Colored beads

A BRILLIANT VARIANT on the bright circus big top, this tablecloth would not be out of place in a maharaja's palace. It exploits the mutable, light-catching qualities of shot silk; every fold glows with resonant color, and its rainbow of fringes gives it a lighthearted charm. If frayed edges are not your style, you could achieve a similar look by using lengths of knotted ribbon. If the thought of centering the smaller circle stops you cold, you could omit it completely and still create a very special tablecover.

Cloth of Many Colors

This is your chance to revel in the pleasure of pure unalloyed color, to assemble a subtle palette, and to display it to glorious advantage. The cutting is easy; the stitching takes patience.

CUTTING AND APPLIQUÉ

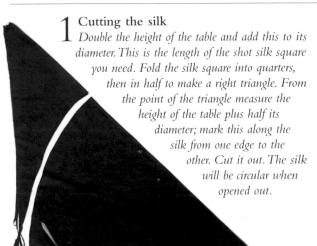

1 Cutting the silk
Double the height of the table and add this to its diameter. This is the length of the shot silk square you need. Fold the silk square into quarters, then in half to make a right triangle. From the point of the triangle measure the height of the table plus half its diameter; mark this along the silk from one edge to the other. Cut it out. The silk will be circular when opened out.

Height of table plus half the diameter

2 Positioning appliqué motifs
Place colored silk triangles backed with fusible webbing (see page 38) all around the silk circle, 1in (2.5cm) in from the edge, with the points facing inward. Peel off the webbing backing paper and iron the triangle in place.

3 Stitching the motifs
Using a sewing machine threaded with multicolored rayon thread, stitch the triangles to the silk with a line of straight stitching around the sides.

APPLYING THE FRINGE

1 Stitching the fringe
Tear pieces of colored silk, organza, and chiffon into small strips. Pin these on top of the triangles with the raw edges even with the edge of the circle. Stitch in place about ½ in (12mm) in from the edge of the silk circle. Remove the pins.

2 Lining the cloth
Cut out polyester lining the same size as the silk. Pin to the silk, sandwiching the strips. Stitch in place. Leave a gap to turn the fabric through. Remove the pins. Turn the tablecloth right side out, then stitch the gap closed. Press.

3 Adding beads
Make a smaller cloth in the same way as above, but leave off the triangles. Tie some beads to the end of some of the strips, then hand-stitch more beads to the edge of the cloth. Sew the smaller cloth to the center of the larger one.

CRACKLED LAMP BASE

MATERIALS

- Wooden lamp base
- Mulberry latex paint
- Acrylic water-based varnish
- Gold acrylic paint
- Two-part crackle varnish
- Gold oil paint
- Oil-based varnish

RICH, DARK COLORS, with a discreet haze of antiqued gold, contribute a classic dignity to a table lamp. The shape has a vague look of the Empire about it, and you could do worse than partner it with a thick cream shade of handmade paper sporting a stenciled laurel wreath. The nimble-fingered could attach the paper shade to the frame with mulberry cord and tassels.

A simple finish, such as the one shown here, is manageable on such a curvaceous shape, whereas stencils, other than the tiniest of motifs, would be tricky. It is perfectly possible, if you have a steady hand, to achieve something more ambitious by painting on freehand bands, stripes, or dots.

Bands of Gold

Subtle gilding enlivens the somber good looks of this lamp base. The effect is formal – a matching pair would radiate gravitas as well as twice the wattage. You could echo the colors elsewhere to make a harmonious theme – in other lamps, in frames, or boxes – to be picked up with upholstery fabrics and cushions.

DECORATING THE BASE

1 Applying the undercoat
Paint the base with two coats of mulberry paint. When dry, apply acrylic water-based varnish to seal.

2 Painting gold decoration
Using an artist's brush, paint rings of gold acrylic paint around the lamp base, following the shape of the molding. Allow to dry.

3 Applying crackle varnish
Apply the first solution of crackle varnish. Let dry, following the manufacturer's instructions. Using a soft-haired synthetic brush, apply the second solution of crackle varnish; let dry.

4 Rubbing in paint
Using a pad of paper towels, gently rub gold oil paint into the cracks that have appeared in the painted surface.

5 Cleaning and varnishing
Using a fresh pad of paper, rub away the paint to reveal the gold cracks beneath. Allow the paint to dry for a few days. Then apply oil-based varnish to seal the surface.

DESIGN OPTION

A Handsome Classic

A graceful lamp base looks beautiful with gold rubbed into the cracks finely and evenly over dark, lustrous green, and burnt umber rubbed into the cracks on gold bands.

FABRIC LAMPSHADE

MATERIALS
- Old lampshade and frame
- Paper
- Upholstery cotton
- PVC backing
- Gold braid
- PVA glue
- Piping cord
- Rayon thread
- Decorative buttons
- Colored raffia

LAMPSHADES ARE AT LAST emerging from the twilight world they have inhabited and coming into the light. For too long they have been the sad embarrassments of any room, quietly gathering dust and serving no other purpose than to hide the bare ignominy of a lightbulb. Lighting is the one crucial element in any room; lampshades are also cheap and very easy to make, and they contribute an instant change of look. You can make shades to match your mood or the season. This tall, conical shape is ideal for the ecologically superior low-energy lightbulbs.

CUTTING OUT

1 Making the template
Carefully peel the shade off an old frame and use this as a template to make a new shade. Lay the shade down flat on a piece of paper. Draw around the edge with a pencil, and then cut out the shape.

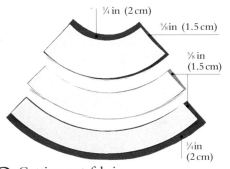

¼ in (2 cm)
⅝ in (1.5 cm)
⅝ in (1.5 cm)
¼ in (2 cm)

2 Cutting out fabric
Cut the paper template into three curved strips. Use these as paper patterns to cut out three pieces of upholstery cotton, adding ¾ in (2 cm) to the top of the smallest strip and to the base of the largest strip, and ⅝ in (1.5 cm) to the right-hand end of each strip of fabric.

3 Adding backing
Lay the fabric pieces facedown, abutting each other. Cut PVC backing the same size as the shade, peel off the paper layer, and lay the backing on the fabric so that the left sides match. Try to be accurate – PVC is very sticky and difficult to reposition.

DECORATING THE LAMPSHADE

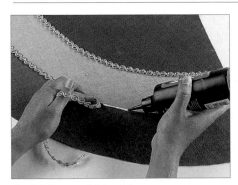

1 Adding gold braid
Turn the fabric right side up. Using PVA glue, attach the gold braid along the fabric joins to conceal them.

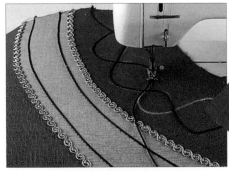

2 Stitching piping lines
Using rayon thread, attach piping cord along the middle of the shade with zigzag stitch. Chalk wavy lines along the top section. Attach piping cord along these lines as before.

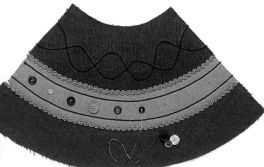

3 Adding buttons
Handstitch decorative buttons along the middle section of the shade, in between the two lines of piping cord.

ASSEMBLING THE LAMPSHADE

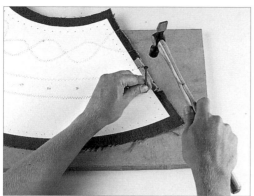

1 **Creating holes for sewing**
Lay the shade, right side down, on a piece of wood. Using a hammer and a large nail, hammer holes through the PVC backing and the fabric around all the edges, about ⅝ in (1.5 cm) apart and about ½ in (1.2 cm) in from the edge.

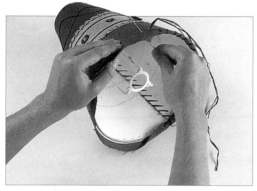

2 **Stitching to the frame**
Thread a large needle with colored raffia and sew the side edges of the shade together. Then insert the frame and oversew around the top and bottom of the frame to secure. Trim fabric if necessary. Use with a low-wattage bulb, between 25 and 40 watts.

Buttons and Braid
This simple but effective lampshade (right) features broad bands of color, accentuated with a flurry of haberdashery in the form of piping cord, Russian braid, raffia, and buttons.

KALEIDOSCOPE CUSHION

MATERIALS

- Paper and cardboard
- 4 20in (50cm) squares of silk or rayon
- Fusible webbing
- 25 x 20in (62.5 x 50cm) gold silk
- Plaid taffeta
- Multicolored rayon thread
- Purple and red silk
- 2 20in (50cm) squares of silk for backing
- 25 x 20in (62.5 x 50cm) cushion pad
- Silk strips for tassels
- Narrow ribbon
- Silk organza

I F YOU HAVE EVER been lured inexorably to the seemingly useless but opulent fabric remnants in a sale, you will find that this cushion cover puts those scraps to perfect use. It is a glamorous example of the whole being far greater than the parts, and can be as elegant and baroque as your scrap bag suggests. If your taste inclines more to natural and countrified, you could adapt the technique for calico and gingham, spotted bandannas and tassels of twine – or go all out for feminine charm and create something rich and luxe from satins, silk, ribbons, and lace. The motifs can be either regular or random – this grid design gives the beginner a comforting sense of structure, but appliqué can be as free as you like.

Harlequin Patches
The appliqués on these cushions (right) draw on a childishly simple repertoire of motifs, but the result is rich and sophisticated.

PREPARING THE FABRIC

1 Cutting templates
Sketch out the design for your cushion on a piece of paper. This simple grid features a combination of stars, spirals, and circles in each square. On a piece of cardboard, draw a star 5in (12.5cm) wide and a circle 3in (7.5cm) in diameter, and cut them out to make templates for the appliquéd shapes.

2 Applying backing
Place a 20in (50cm) silk or rayon square right side down. Lay fusible webbing on top, sticky side down. Run a warm iron over this for a few seconds until the adhesive darkens. Repeat the process on three more squares.

3 Marking motifs
Using a pencil, draw around the star template six times on each of two fabric squares – here a spotted rayon and a rayon print. Then draw around the circle template six times on each of the two remaining squares – here, a plain red silk and a very dark green silk.

4 Cutting out appliqué motifs
Cut out the motifs; the fusible webbing should remain attached. You should now have 12 star and 12 circle motifs.

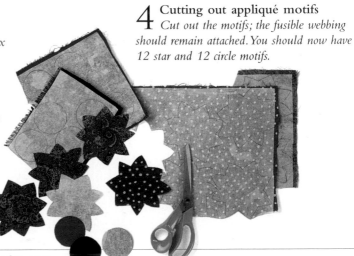

ASSEMBLING THE DESIGN

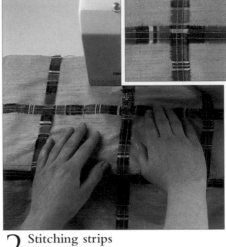

1 Assembling the grid
Lay the 25 x 20 in (62.5 x 50 cm) panel of gold silk down, right side up. Referring to the design sketch, lay three strips of plaid taffeta lengthwise and four strips widthwise across the silk to form a grid with 20 squares. Pin the taffeta strips in place.

2 Stitching strips
Thread a sewing machine with multicolored rayon thread, or colored cotton thread if you prefer. Stitch each strip to the gold silk with two lines of straight stitching (see inset). Remove the pins.

3 Positioning motifs
Arrange the star and circle motifs in the two outer vertical rows and the central vertical row of squares, alternating the different colors of fabric. Peel the fusible webbing paper backing off each motif, then place the motifs in position. Place the circles on top of the stars.

4 Fusing motifs
Iron the motifs in place as you go with a warm iron. The heat melts the webbing and fuses the motifs to the silk. Repeat until all the motifs are attached to the cushion front.

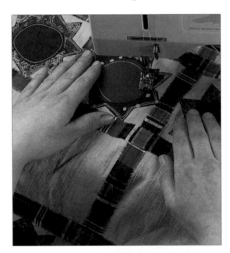

5 Stitching motifs
Using multicolored rayon thread or colored cotton thread, machine-stitch two rows of straight stitching around each star. Then stitch one row of straight stitching around each circle. You could use a darning foot here if you prefer.

6 Stitching silk spirals
Stitch a torn strip of purple silk in a spiral in one of the remaining squares. Then stitch a spiral of torn red silk in the next square. Repeat to fill all the remaining squares of the grid with alternating purple and red silk spirals.

7 Decorating the circles
Stitch a torn strip of red silk in a spiral on top of one of the appliquéd circles. Then stitch a spiral of torn purple silk on the next appliquéd circle. Repeat this process on all the remaining circles, alternating red and purple silk strips as before.

MAKING THE BACKING

1 Positioning backing pieces
Place two 20 in (50 cm) squares of contrasting-colored silk on top of the gold silk, right sides facing the appliqués. The two squares should overlap in the middle. Fold back each overlapping end twice, so that the ends overlap by about 5 in (12.5 cm).

2 Stitching backing
Pin the backing pieces to the gold silk along all four sides. Stitch around the edges with cotton thread. Remove the pins. Turn the cushion cover right side out through the central overlapping flap. Insert a 25 x 20 in (62.5 x 50 cm) cushion pad.

MAKING A TASSEL

For a finishing flourish, add a tassel to each corner of the cushion. They are easy to make with scraps of silk and can be attached using a few hand stitches.

1 Lay a bunch of 10 colored silk strips, 10 in (25 cm) long, on a flat surface. Tie them in the middle with a narrow ribbon or silk strip.

2 Fold the strips in half so that the tied ribbon is at the center. Using a 10 in (25 cm) strip of silk organza, tie a bow around the folded silk strips, about ½ in (12 mm) below the fold.

3 Trim the ends of the silk tassel to the desired length. Repeat to make three more tassels.

DESIGN OPTIONS

Diamond Lattice

Stitched stripes are the base for this small square cushion (below). A grid of strips was stitched diagonally over them and the regular intersections punctuated by giant cross stitches. Against this background, multicolored rosettes were appliquéd, producing an effect that is both formal and spontaneous.

Leaves and Flowers

This cushion (above) appears to have all the carefree spontaneity of a child's drawing, but it has been carefully considered and built up in many layers on a bright patchwork of colors. Hand stitching is a strong element of this design.

Patches and Petals

The foundation for this medium-sized square cushion (left) is a silk patchwork consisting of a central block surrounded by 12 smaller squares. A regular lattice of fabric strips has been stitched over this from corner to corner and the resulting diamonds have been filled with spirals of alternating purple and gold, and random shaggy flowers.

GILDED CHESSBOARD

MATERIALS

- 18 in (45 cm) square of medium density fiberboard (MDF),
- Latex paint: mulberry, off-white
- Masking tape
- Acrylic water-based varnish
- Low-tack tape
- Acrylic gold size
- Transfer Dutch metal leaf
- Shellac

FOR SOME, CHESS IS a matter of life or death, mirroring the complex battles of the world at large; such players do not want to be distracted from their strategic pursuit by ostentation. This sober and dignified chessboard is the very thing for such serious players, with its field of ivory and gold, bordered with maroon.

By far the most taxing aspect of making the board is the calculation required for the grid of squares. This momentary challenge aside, there is nothing to stop you from having a suite of chessboards in different colors to match your mood and to instill optimism.

PREPARING THE BOARD

1 Applying the paint
Using a paint roller, paint the MDF square with two coats of mulberry latex paint. Allow to dry. Mask off a 1 in (2.5 cm) border around the edge. Paint a coat of off-white latex on top. Allow to dry.

2 Sanding the surface
Rub sandpaper wrapped around a sanding block over the painted square in a circular motion to reveal some of the base coat. Brush away the dust. Apply two coats of acrylic water-based varnish, and let dry.

Field of Gold
For those of us who always lose at chess, there is some small consolation in playing on a board (right) that is the result of your own artistic efforts.

3 Drawing the squares
Using a ruler and pencil, mark lines vertically and horizontally across the painted square, spaced 2 in (5 cm) apart.

4 Masking the squares
Using low-tack tape, mask off alternate horizontal and vertical squares. Make sure the tape lies straight along the penciled lines.

GILDING THE BOARD

1 Applying metal leaf
Brush acrylic gold size on the masked squares. Lay the transfer Dutch metal leaf onto each square in turn. Press the backing paper with a fingernail for a neat edge (see inset); rub the leaf gently. Peel off the backing paper. Burnish the gilded squares with a cotton ball.

2 Varnishing
Brush shellac onto the gold squares to tone down the brightness; allow to dry. Brush acrylic water-based varnish over the gold squares to seal. When dry, peel off the tape and mask off the remaining squares. Gild these in the same way.

3 Adding texture
Peel off all the tape; this will lift up some of the varnish on the gilded squares. Stick a piece of tape over each gilded square, then peel it off. This will lift up a little more of the varnish, giving a textured finish. Finally, apply a coat of varnish.

DECORATIVE EXTRAS

THERE ARE MANY other games besides chess, fortunately for those of us who always lose at it. Many who combine game playing with a passion for collecting are well aware that a handsome board takes one vastly closer to enjoying any game, and the board can be an admirable object in its own right. Making game boards gives all the pleasures of fine art, while requiring none of the skill. It is a tremendous way to flex your decorative muscles.

Simple geometric patterns, such as squares and triangles, do not require genius or inspiration, and you can be as irreverent as you like with your choice of colors and materials. If you want to use a collage of different-colored wine labels, or a collection of playing cards, go ahead; the only limit is your imagination. Chess, checkers, and backgammon can all be deadly serious, but a light-hearted approach takes some of the sting out of the playing.

Backgammon Duo

An attempt at creating the look of the family heirloom provides an enjoyable exercise in innocent fraud. There are various ways to achieve the antiqued finishes of these two game boards.

• *Rub a candle over the base coat, then stencil triangles on top. Distress this paintwork with steel wool for an antiqued look. Alternatively, apply crackle glaze over the painted surface for a network of fine cracks.*

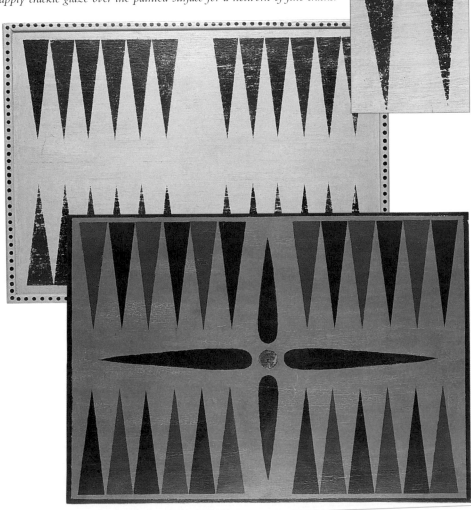

Country Inspirations

This design is a piece of unashamed plagiarism in homage to the feisty passion for game boards; the rich sonorous colors in neat squares with a crisp banded edging will be familiar to anyone who has studied country interiors.

• *To make this square chessboard, stencil indigo squares onto a board of red-painted medium density fiberboard (MDF). Add a border of indigo and ocher using masking tape as a guide. Seal with matte varnish.*

Trompe-l'oeil Chessboard

This folding table is decorated with squares stenciled with a sponge, with découpaged Italian playing cards, postcards, and a coin, and with simple trompe-l'oeil dice, checkers, and dominoes. *Trompe-l'oeil* is not actually difficult at this level, but it is fascinating, absorbing, and rewarding. Don't lose courage if you think the fake objects look ridiculously unconvincing as you paint them. Keep referring to the actual objects, and observing the effects of light and shade. Before you know it, the whole thing will spring to three-dimensional life before your eyes.

• *Stencil terra-cotta and indigo squares onto an ocher ground, then decorate the edges with a combination of découpage tarot cards and simple acrylic trompe-l'oeil game pieces. Try out your collage first, using a strong single light source. Then draw or trace the final position of your fake objects, together with the shadows they cast. Using carbon paper, transfer the layout of the shadows to the chessboard. Then antique the board with craquelure and burnt umber oil paint.*

Paper Squares

If you are a natural iconoclast, it will give you a secret thrill of pleasure to dismay the fusty chess-playing fraternity by making a board that flaunts four colors instead of the legislated two. This board was made with wonderful tissue-fine handmade Indian paper, in subtle shades of light pink, beige, dark forest green, and indigo. The tones of light and dark contrast sufficiently to make the board work. With all these effects it is wise to varnish the finished board for protection.

• *Using PVA glue, stick squares of handmade paper onto a penciled grid marked on an ocher-painted board. Then apply a coat of craquelure over the surface and burnish this with burnt umber oil paint.*

APPLIQUÉ PELMET

MATERIALS
- Interfacing
- Silk
- Sewing thread
- Remnants of colored silk
- Fusible webbing
- Multicolored rayon thread
- Colored beads
- Tassels *(see page 41)*
- Touch-and-close tape

N O FABRIC CAN beat silk for luxury – nothing comes close for sumptuous texture and intense color. This pelmet, with its festive pennants and heraldic motifs, is like something from medieval pageantry, but the technique could easily find as many different expressions as there are fabrics. Somber silks and velvets, for example, could be magnificent in a porticoed and pillared plantation house, while gingham and madras cotton with appliquéd suns, stars, and bright ribbon tassels would bring year-round cheer to a baby's bedroom.

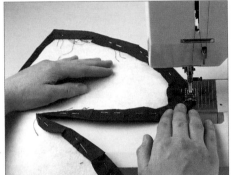

MAKING THE PELMET

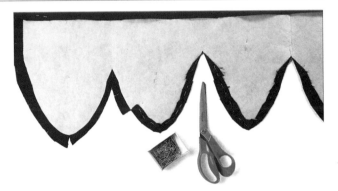

1 Cutting interfacing
Cut a strip the width of the window by 12 in (30 cm). Fold lengthwise, in accordion folds. Draw a half-scallop from the folded edge to the opposite edge, and cut along this line.

2 Pinning silk to interfacing
Open out the interfacing. Pin the cut-out interfacing to a length of silk and cut out the silk following the shape of the interfacing, about 1 in (2.5 cm) wider all around. Turn over all the edges of the silk and pin them to the interfacing, snipping the curved edges to create an even finish.

3 Stitching the silk
Using a sewing machine with a straight stitch, and with matching-colored thread in the bobbin, stitch the silk to the interfacing around all the pinned edges. Remove the pins.

Window Dressing
A glorious confection of silk tassels and scallops, this pelmet is easily made and simple to attach. You may even consider turning out a repertoire of different looks to suit the seasons, with matching pillows to boot, if the impulse strikes you.

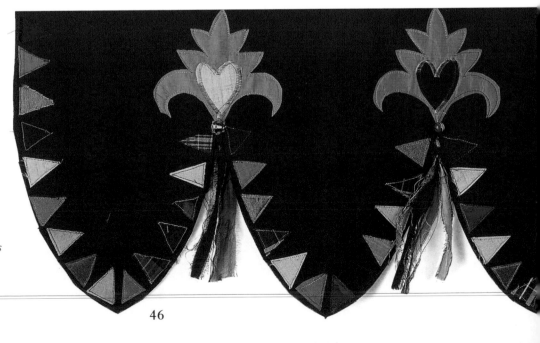

APPLYING FABRIC SHAPES

2 Stitching motifs
With multicolored rayon thread in the sewing machine, stitch the motifs to the pelmet. Stitch the triangles and floral motifs around their edges with straight stitch, then stitch a heart inside each floral motif with zigzag stitch around the edges. If you prefer, use a darning foot on your machine for this stage; it makes stitching easier.

1 Positioning appliqué motifs
Turn the pelmet silk side up. Cut silk triangles and floral motifs; back them with fusible webbing (see page 38). Position the triangles around the scallops and the floral motifs between scallops. Peel off the fusible webbing backing paper and iron in place.

3 Attaching tassels
Hand-stitch a bead and tassel (see page 41) between each scallop. Place the top of the tassel behind the pelmet and stitch it to the pelmet, then take the thread through to the right side of the pelmet to stitch down a bead. Repeat with a few stitches to secure the tassel and the bead. Attach the pelmet to the window frame with self-adhesive touch-and-close tape.

PATCHWORK THROW

MATERIALS

- Assorted pieces of cotton or wool
- Fusible webbing
- Sewing thread
- Cotton backing fabric, 56 in (140 cm) square

THIS COZY, COUNTRY THROW in strong autumn colors is reminiscent of pine woods, wild daisies, and a sprinkling of russet leaves. A practical, washable cotton throw has a thousand uses. In a household with children, it will do hard service fulfilling functions as diverse as a post-bathtime wrap and spaceship walls. For adults, a throw might adorn a tabletop, brighten a sofa, or be spread on the floor in front of the fire for impromptu picnics. The appliqué pattern can be cut from paper folded in quarters to make a template and, for anyone in a hurry, the flowers and leaves can be attached with machine zigzag stitching.

DESIGN OPTIONS

Cozy Throw

A light cotton or woolen throw is a wonderfully easy way to bring color and softness to the most spartan living room.

Color Combinations

Bold handstitching and loose informality of design, combined with patchwork and embroidery, yield an appealingly casual look. Thick, airy wool is cut into random shapes whose blanket-stitched edges are part of the design. The linen lemons can be positioned by tacking or fusible webbing, and stitched by hand or machine.

CUTTING OUT

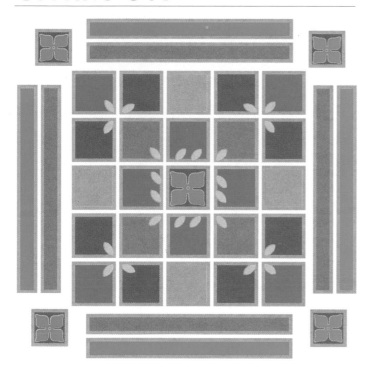

2 Stitching motifs
Using a needle and sewing thread, stitch the five flower motifs onto separate cotton squares; blanket stitch around the edges.

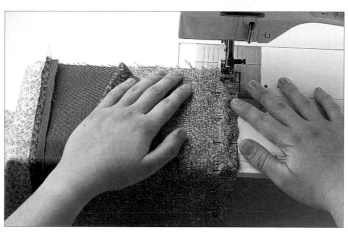

1 Cutting out fabric
Cut out 29 squares of cotton fabric, each measuring 8in (20cm). This design is made of 13 mauve, 8 green, and 4 each purple and pink patterned squares. Then cut out 4 strips each of green and purple patterned fabric, each measuring 4 x 40in (10cm x 1m). Finally cut out 5 flower motifs from cotton, after first backing them with fusible webbing (see page 38).

3 Assembling the design
Arrange the squares in a large square design, five squares long. Position an appliquéd square in the center. Pin and machine-stitch the patches together, using a ⅝in (1.5cm) seam. Stitch the border strips around the edges and stitch an appliquéd square in each corner.

ADDING DECORATION AND FINISHING

1 Adding decorative motifs
Cut out several leaf shapes from cotton fabric, after first backing the cotton with fusible webbing (see page 38). Position the shapes around the central appliquéd flower and in groups of three around the throw. Iron and then stitch the shapes to the throw using tiny catch stitches.

2 Stitching backing
Sew a cotton backing onto the throw to conceal all the stitching. To do this, place the backing fabric on the throw, right sides together, then machine stitch all around the edge. Leave a small gap on one side. Turn the throw right side out through the gap, press, then slipstitch the gap closed.

THE
DINING
ROOM

DÉCOUPAGE DOOR PLATE

·

PRINTED TABLECLOTH

·

QUILTED PLACE MAT

·

GILDED CANDLESTICKS

·

NEEDLEPOINT CUSHION

·

IDEAS FOR CHRISTMAS

DÉCOUPAGE DOOR PLATE

MATERIALS
- Black-and-white illustration
- Glass door plate
- Tea bag
- Water
- Shellac
- PVA glue
- Acrylic gold size
- Transfer Dutch metal leaf
- Gold acrylic paint

A SIMPLE MEANS TO BRING A TOUCH of grandeur to your dining room door and discreetly keep finger marks at bay, this découpaged and gilded door plate is one of those small but significant details that make a house infinitely more interesting. People who like their surroundings plain can take up residence in an Amish barn. Those of us who enjoy a touch of the baroque, a glimpse of the rococo, and a whiff of style and luxury are never as happy as when adding a few completely unnecessary decorative flourishes to the plainly functional.

PREPARING THE DÉCOUPAGE

1 Staining the photocopy
Find a black and white illustration to fit your door plate; photocopy it. Stain the copy pale brown by wiping a wet tea bag over it a few times. Let it dry for 15 minutes.

2 Sealing with shellac
Using a pad of paper towels, wipe shellac over the back of the paper. This will seal the paper and prevent it from disintegrating when it is being glued to the door plate.

3 Cutting out
When the shellac is dry (about 2 minutes), cut out the black and white illustration using manicure scissors. You can use a scalpel if you prefer, but remember to protect your work surface with a cutting mat or piece of thick cardboard.

APPLYING THE DESIGN AND GILDING

1 Marking the door plate
Place the cutout illustration right side up. Center the glass door plate over it. Using a marker, mark the outline of the illustration on the glass.

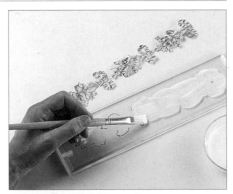

2 Gluing the door plate
Turn the door plate over and brush PVA glue over the surface to cover the area of the illustration.

3 Positioning the design
Lay the illustration facedown on the glued glass. Turn the door plate over and move the illustration around until it is positioned within the marked outline. Press the illustration with a sponge to remove any air bubbles.

4 Applying gold size
Brush acrylic gold size over the reverse side of the door plate. Leave it for 15 to 20 minutes, when it should turn clear and become tacky.

5 Applying gold leaf
Lay a piece of transfer metal leaf over the tacky size. Rub it down gently with a cotton ball and remove the backing paper. Repeat to gild the rest of the door plate.

6 Applying gold paint
Using a soft brush, apply gold acrylic paint over the metal leaf. This will hide any scratches in the leaf when you view the door plate from the front. Allow to dry and attach to the door.

Gold Plate
A finger plate was once considered essential for every well-dressed door, and this easy combination of découpage and gilding gives a finishing touch of antique gravitas. It could be complemented by a faceted glass doorknob.

PRINTED TABLECLOTH

MATERIALS
- White cotton fabric
- Screen printing inks (iron fixable)
- Potato
- Sewing thread

THIS IS ABOUT AS BASIC as you can get – you probably did potato prints in nursery school – but by using a vibrant mix of colors and massing the moderately complicated design into close, serried rows, you get a richly textured effect. Neither method nor materials are unduly demanding, and you could enlist the help of younger family members, replacing your potatoes with fresh cuts as they lose their edge. With the huge spectrum of iron–fixable printing inks to draw upon, and the endlessly adaptable printing method, there is no limit to the effects you can achieve.

Printed with Panache
This tablecloth has a carefree Mediterranean air, but if you printed in earthy umbers and black onto clay-brown cloth, you could dream of Africa; ochers, cream, and cinnabar red could evoke Morocco.

DECORATING THE FABRIC

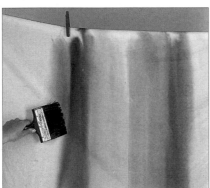

2 Carving the potato
Using a small, sharp knife, cut a medium-sized potato in half and carve a design into one of the halves to make a printing block. When you print with the block, the raised areas will be visible. Blot the cut surface of the potato with paper towels to absorb any excess moisture.

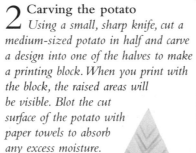

1 Painting the cotton
Wash the fabric and hang it on a line. Using a housepainter's brush, daub vertical lines of screen printing ink all over the wet fabric. The colors will merge and become blurred. When dry, iron the fabric on the right side with a hot iron to fix the inks.

3 Inking up a sponge
Ink up a thin, smooth sponge cloth by applying screen printing ink to its surface with a spatula. Apply a few colors onto the sponge cloth together, so that some of the colors overlap.

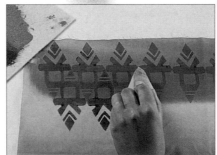

4 Inking the potato
To ink up the potato block, press the carved half of the potato evenly onto the inked sponge cloth. When you lift it up you will see the raised area of the potato covered with ink.

5 Printing on the fabric
Press the inked potato onto the painted fabric, starting at the top left and working in rows across the fabric. Turn the potato upside down for the second row and position it between the first and second prints of the row above to create an interlocking pattern.

6 Varying the pattern
Continue to print horizontal rows, varying the placing of the potato and changing color as you go. Leave the completed design to dry for 24 hours. Iron it on the front and back to fix the inks. Then hem all four edges to complete the tablecloth.

QUILTED PLACE MAT

MATERIALS

- Lining fabric
- Cotton print fabric
- Sewing thread: yellow, orange, rust-red
- Assorted remnants of colored polyester
- Fusible webbing
- Cardboard heart templates
- ¼ in (6 mm) batting
- Orange cotton fabric
- Lining fabric for backing

ONCE UPON A TIME, no meal was properly dressed unless there was a whole panoply of tablecloths, mats, napkins, napkin rings, coasters, and 23 varieties of cutlery. Fortunately, those days are gone, and we can now indulge in the luxury of choice – every now and then it is just festive and fun to deck your dinner table with a few additional touches of original linens. These quilted mats will forgive a flattened soufflé and fulfill the practical function of protecting your table finish from hot plates. It makes sense to choose your fabrics with washability in mind so that your mats do not become a culinary journal.

Hearty Meals

A feast of luscious color and exuberant design is guaranteed to bring the often overlooked and undervalued ingredient of finesse to your dining room.

ASSEMBLING THE GRID

1 Assembling the fabric
Cut out a rectangle of lining fabric measuring approximately 17 x 13 in (42.5 x 32.5 cm). Tear strips of cotton print fabric ½ in (12 mm) wide and the length or width of the rectangle. Lay them on the rectangle to form a grid pattern consisting of six squares. Pin into position.

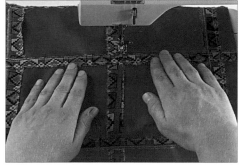

2 Stitching the grid strips
Using yellow sewing thread, machine-stitch the grid strips into position with two rows of straight stitching. Remove the pins.

ADDING DECORATION

1 Cutting out motifs
Back three small pieces of colored polyester with fusible webbing (see page 38). Using cardboard templates, cut out one large and one small heart from each piece. Peel off the fusible webbing paper backing and iron the hearts onto the grid, alternating the colors in each square.

2 Stitching motifs
Cut out a piece of batting the same size as the fabric rectangle; pin the fabric to this. Using a darning foot on the machine and with the presser foot down, stitch the hearts to the fabric rectangle with a straight stitch around the edges, using orange sewing thread.

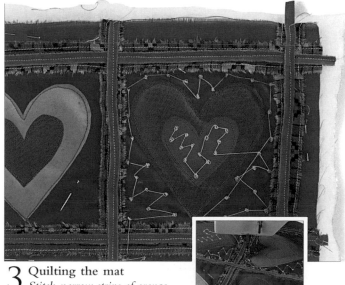

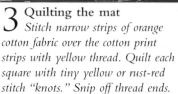

3 Quilting the mat
Stitch narrow strips of orange cotton fabric over the cotton print strips with yellow thread. Quilt each square with tiny yellow or rust-red stitch "knots." Snip off thread ends.

4 Backing the mat
Stitch squares of ocher polyester over each grid intersection. Stitch backing fabric to the table mat, right sides together, leaving a gap. Turn right side out; slipstitch the gap closed.

GILDED CANDLESTICKS

MATERIALS

- 2 wooden candlesticks
- Latex paint in two shades of green
- Acrylic water-based varnish
- Gilt cream

THE MOST DIFFICULT ASPECT of decorating these candlesticks is finding plain wooden blanks in the first place – the rest is child's play. The combination of ragging and gilt cream gives plenty of texture and brings out the details of the wood turning. Touches of gold or metallic cream, like pieces of mirror mosaic and strips or studs of metal, all add to the reflective quality of candlesticks and shimmer in response to a dancing flame. Candlesticks are so easy to decorate that you could have a collection of special occasion ones to bring out for Christmas and birthday celebrations. Painting and gilding to match is the perfect way to make a diverse collection of junk store discoveries work together, the more shapes and sizes the better; an assortment of different heights always looks good.

Light Touch

These candlesticks bring a festive and subtly stately air to your dining room – they are quick and easy to make, and look good in groups.

PAINTING THE CANDLESTICKS

1 Applying the base coat
Using a small paintbrush, paint each candlestick with a coat of the lighter green latex paint, and let dry.

2 Painting the second color
Paint a coat of darker green latex paint over each candlestick, applying the paint quickly.

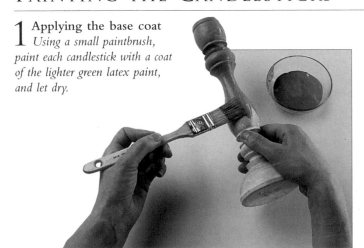

3 Ragging the candlesticks
Dab a scrunched-up cotton rag over the wet paint. This will lift off some of the darker green paint and reveal patches of the base color, adding texture to the decoration.

4 Varnishing the surface
Allow the candlesticks to dry, then apply a coat of acrylic water-based varnish to seal the surface. Let dry.

5 Applying gilt cream
Rub gilt cream over parts of each candlestick with a finger. When dry, buff with a soft cloth for a slight sheen.

NEEDLEPOINT CUSHION

MATERIALS

- 12 in (30 cm) square of 18-count evenweave fabric
- Embroidery threads
- 16 in (40 cm) square of lightweight calico
- 4 strips of green cotton, 1 x 16 in (2.5 x 40 cm)
- Matching sewing thread
- 16 strips of green, and 4 strips of gold cotton, 16 x 1½ in (40 x 4 cm)
- Backing fabric
- 10 strips of backing cotton 16 x 1–2 in (40 x 2.5–5 cm)
- 8 strips of cotton for ties, 10 x 1½ in (25 x 4 cm)
- Piping cord
- Cushion pad to fit

NEEDLEPOINT IS THE PASTIME *par excellence* for precise and fastidious perfectionists, be they stressed-out executives for whom it is calming, or languid lotus eaters to whom it gives a sense of purpose, not to mention a covetable cushion cover. Needlepoint is portable, and it is really difficult to make a mistake. Should your stitching efforts finish up as a wayward parallelogram, you can easily rectify the problem and turn it into a neat square by ironing it with a steam iron. Then you can frame it, or, if you feel creative, make a cleverly shaded cushion cover from it. The same design could be worked on finer fabric as a *petit point* pincushion, or in thick wool or fabric strips to become a rug. An exploration of your local craft or sewing shop will unearth a surprising number of grades of canvas and thicknesses of tapestry yarn.

Stitched Prism

A passing reference to the classic Flying Geese patchwork design in the stitching and Log Cabin piecing in the surround give a whiff of tradition to this geometric needlepoint design in fiery autumn colors.

MAKING THE CENTRAL PANEL

1 Beginning the stitching
Stretch the evenweave fabric on a frame, pinning each side to the frame with silk pins to keep it drum-tight. Thread a tapestry needle with embroidery thread and, using the template (see page 219), begin stitching in the center of the design with half cross stitch. To do this, take the needle down near the center of the fabric, leaving a long end of thread on the surface. Bring the needle up through the central hole (see inset), then take it down the hole to the top right of this one to work a diagonal stitch. Bring the needle up through the hole directly beneath to start the next half cross stitch.

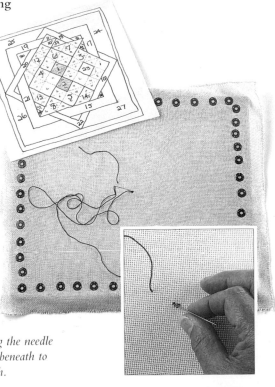

2 Working the pattern
Continue to work half cross stitches in this way, following the template. Ensure that you maintain the same diagonal slope with all the stitches to achieve the textural quality.

3 Completing the design
As you work more colors, you will see the design taking shape. When you have completed the needlepoint, remove it from the frame.

MAKING THE CUSHION FRONT

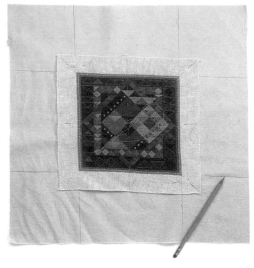

2 Marking pencil lines

Mark on the calico two pencil lines starting from each point of the needlepoint and going to the outer edge, horizontally and vertically. These act a guidelines for stitching the first patchwork strips in place.

1 Basting guidelines

Lay the needlepoint right side up on the calico, ensuring it is centered. Pin in place, then baste with colored thread, starting from the center of the needlepoint and working outward to each corner.

3 Edging with fabric

With right sides together, pin two strips of cotton, 1 in (2.5 cm) wide, to opposite sides of the needlepoint square. Place the strips so that the stitching will align with the pencil marks. Stitch in place, allowing a small seam. Press each set of two strips back over the seam before adding the next two strips.

4 Stitching log cabin strips

Continue to stitch 1¹/₂ in (4cm) wide strips of cotton around the four sides of the needlepoint to build up a log-cabin effect. The strips will become longer the farther away they are from the needlepoint, and should graduate from light to dark green. Continue until you have covered all the calico background.

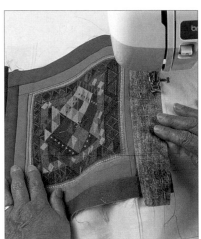

MAKING THE BACKING AND FINISHING THE CUSHION

1 Piecing the backing

The backing comprises two pieces of fabric, each overlaid with several strips of cotton. One should measure 16 x 8in (40 x 20cm) and the other 16 x 15in (40 x 38cm). Stitch several strips of cotton to each piece, each strip being 16in (40cm) long and a variety of widths. Press each strip over to cover the seam before basting the next one in place. Make a 1¹/₁₆in (1.5cm) hem on one 16in (40cm) edge on each backing piece; turn under an extra 3⁹/₁₆ in (9cm) on the larger piece.

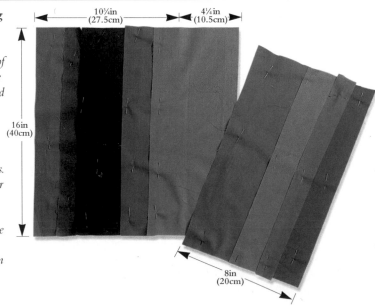

10¾in (27.5cm)   4¼in (10.5cm)

16in (40cm)

8in (20cm)

2 Attaching ties

Make four cushion ties. For a tie, machine stitch together two strips of cotton around four sides, leaving a gap. Turn right side out and slipstitch the gap closed. Lay the backing pieces flat so that they overlap in the center by 2⅛ in (6cm). Position the ties opposite one another, with two on each side of the overlap. Machine in place.

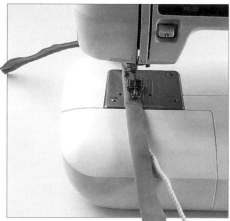

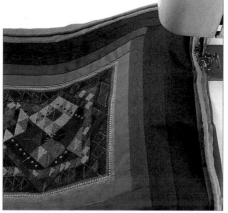

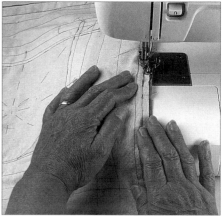

3 **Making piping**
Cut four lengths of gold-colored cotton 1½ in (4 cm) wide and slightly longer than the cushion sides. Cut piping cord to match. Fold the fabric over each piece of cord and stitch close to the cord, using a zipper foot.

4 **Attaching piping**
Pin and baste the piping strips to the edges of the right side of the cushion with raw edges matching. Machine stitch in place using the zipper foot on the machine.

5 **Attaching cushion backing**
Lay the front cover of the cushion over the back sections, right sides together. Baste, and then machine, around the edges. Be careful not to trap the ties. Turn the cover the right way out through the back opening. Insert a cushion pad.

DESIGN OPTIONS

Burgundy and Slate

The kaleidoscope effect of spinning squares and triangles (above) is more dramatic in this version of the original design, and the dark log-cabin frame completes the look.

Country Palette

The quiet muted blues and peachy browns of this cover (above right) are reminiscent of brooding skies, wind-whipped seas, wild roses, and plowed fields, making a fascinating mixture of colors to muse upon. The back continues the color theme with classic detailing (top right).

IDEAS FOR CHRISTMAS

CHRISTMAS DOES NOT HAVE to mean kitsch, although that has its charms, too. With coordination and a little thought, the usual chaos can be kept in check; at least your contribution can be stylish, even if everyone else on the planet seems to have gone mad. Take a handful of classic Christmas images – this is not the time for outrageous originality; just make sure your holly, ivy, and stars are better than anyone else's – and make them a leitmotif for wrapping paper, cards, and decoration. If you stick to black, white, and red, with the odd foray into more exotic colors for wrapping paper, it will help establish a theme. This Christmas collection is composed of a fistful of good-looking and simple ideas – your children may be terrific allies for many of these operations, for a minute or two at least. Think classy and festive, begin in August, and you should be ready for the fray.

WRAPPING PAPER

This is ordinary wrapping paper printed with random stars, using a modest potato. Kid's stuff. It does take time, and it helps if every Christmas bundle's a neat cube, but the general principle cannot be beaten. Try different kinds of paper – plain brown paper looks terrific printed, as does tissue paper. One of the joys is that you can spend your hard-earned money on the presents themselves rather than on the wrapping.

Colored ribbon bow

Assorted colored paper

Roller

Gold acrylic paint

White latex paint

Star potato block

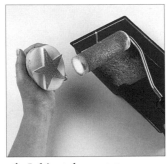

1 Inking the potato
Cut a potato in half and carve a star in the cut surface. Blot with a paper towel. Using a paint roller, ink up the potato printing block with gold paint.

2 Printing with the potato
Press the potato printing block evenly onto a piece of paper, then lift it up to reveal the star print. Repeat to print gold stars all over the paper.

CAKE BOX

What more elegant excuse to increase somebody else's waistline than to give them a snowy iced Christmas cake or pretty cookies in a very classy box? Dispatching the contents will be a matter of moments, but the box will linger on, put to all sorts of other uses. Using wonderful hand-written manuscripts – photocopied if the originals are too precious to part with – is a speedy and cunning way to make an instant designer object.

• *Photocopy your chosen paper and cut it out to the correct size for the surface of the box. Brush a thin layer of PVA glue over each side of the box in turn, and carefully stick down the paper, smoothing it out to remove any air bubbles.*

CHRISTMAS CARDS

MATERIALS FOR CAKE BOX
AND CHRISTMAS CARDS

Pressed leaves

Ribbon

Watercolor paper

Photocopied script

Ribbon

Tissue paper

Dutch metal leaf

Flat-backed glass nuggets

PVA glue and brush

In the frantic time-juggling rush toward Christmas, nothing stops you dead in your tracks quite like a beautifully handmade Christmas card. And if you think about it, it is perfectly possible to make your own – pragmatically it might be quicker. These cards are unsurpassable and bear a fascinating hoard of script, silk gauze, glass baubles, and dried leaves. When using this kind of material, it helps to be as neat and accurate as you can – crisp perfection in cutting and gluing is what you should aim for. Making treasurable cards is not difficult: learn to trust your eye, and PVA glue.

1 Building up layers
Tear a rectangle of watercolor paper. Fold it in half to make a card. Using PVA glue, stick torn photocopied script onto the front of the card. Then glue a square of Dutch metal leaf on top. Stick a pressed oak leaf on top of the gold square.

2 Adding glass nugget
Apply PVA glue to the back of a flat-backed glass nugget and stick this on the front of the card. Let dry.

SPARKLING CANDELABRA

A miser's hoard of glittering crystal droplets picked up at a garage sale was the starting point for this superb exercise in thrifty customizing. A black iron rope-work chandelier was gilded using gilt cream. The faceted glass, simply threaded onto gold and silver wire and hung on its branches, catches the light with every movement of air and sheds a spectrum or two in favorable circumstances.

Applying gilt cream
Dip your finger into a pot of gilt cream and rub it all over the candelabra, working it well into the grooves. Let dry before fixing on the glass droplets with wire.

MATERIALS FOR CANDELABRA AND CANDLESTICK

Holly and ivy leaves

Gilt cream

Fuse wire

Bronze foil

Pencil

Copper foil

Crystal droplets

Foil cutters

FOIL LEAF CANDLESTICK

Holly and ivy leaves, cut somewhat painfully from bronze and copper foil, make a shimmering halo around five glowing candles. This must be the simplest way to bring light and glamour to a Christmas dining table. Like the crystal droplets, these leaves move in every current of air, making a lively and festive table centerpiece.

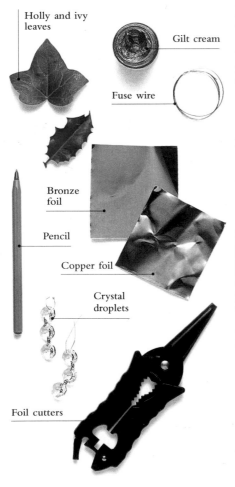

Wiring the leaf shapes
After cutting out the holly and ivy leaf shapes from bronze and copper foil, twist fuse wire around the stalks, and then wrap the ends of the wire around the arms of the candlestick to secure.

CHRISTMAS ALBUM

It is all too easy to forget who gave what to whom, what everybody ate, and what games were played at Christmas unless you keep a Christmas diary in which to log events, stick photos and cards, and record menus with notes on successes and failures.

• *Glue wrapping paper over the outside of a notebook (see page 93). Add colored paper on the spine and corners. Finally, glue a Santa motif in the center.*

Colored plain paper

Wrapping paper

Santa motifs

TWINKLING TWIG TREE

A sophisticated home for your Christmas lights can be made from willow or hazel twigs, hung with citrus fruit dried to subtle colors and held in place with seashore pebbles or gravel. A duo of old terra-cotta pots, tied with a wide gold paper bow, makes a handsome container. A variant might be a larger dead branch, with scintillas of light tied in place with plain satin or tartan ribbon bows.

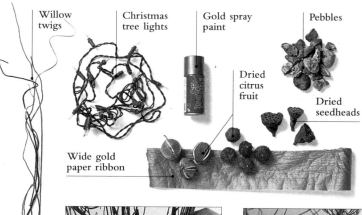

Willow twigs

Christmas tree lights

Gold spray paint

Pebbles

Dried citrus fruit

Dried seedheads

Wide gold paper ribbon

Simple Still Life
A minimalist, yet extremely effective, Christmas decoration.

1 Arranging twigs
Fill a pot with pebbles, then arrange twigs in the pot, wedging them into position. Spray the wire of the Christmas lights gold.

2 Attaching the lights
When dry, arrange the Christmas lights around the twigs. Secure them in place with pieces of fuse wire.

3 Hanging the decorations
Cover the pebbles with dried seedheads and tie a gold paper bow around the pot. Hang dried citrus fruits from the twigs.

THE KITCHEN

PAINTED KITCHEN CLOCK

MATERIALS

- Medium density fiberboard (MDF) or wooden clock
- White latex paint
- Decorative image
- Tracing paper
- Masking tape
- Transfer/carbon paper
- Sheet of clock numbers (available at craft stores)
- Fine-tipped blue waterproof marker
- Blue acrylic paint
- Acrylic water-based varnish
- Clock movement

INEXPENSIVE QUARTZ CLOCK movements can be bought by mail order from many hobby shops, and since they incorporate hands, battery, and hanging device, all you need to provide is a flat front upon which to paint the face. In other words, cheap technology means that you can make a clock face out of just about anything flat that suits your fancy – a strip of wood found on the beach, a sheet of rusted metal, a laminated black and white photograph, an elegant rectangular Japanese lacquer mat, a page of newspaper glued onto heavy cardboard and pasted with large cutout numerals in different typefaces and varnished, or best of all, one of the cheap precut MDF blanks you can use to give your imagination full rein. You could make a paper collage or use any paint effect you like.

PREPARING THE CLOCK

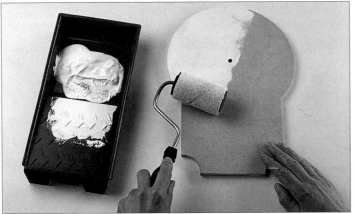

1 Painting the clock
Using a roller, apply two coats of white latex paint over the front and sides of the clock, allowing the first coat to dry before applying the second. Let dry.

2 Drawing the border
Tape a piece of cardboard over the clock movement hole in the center of the clock to give you some purchase for your compass point. Using a pair of compasses, draw a pencil circle around the clock face ¼ in (6 mm) in from the edge. This gives you a narrow border to decorate.

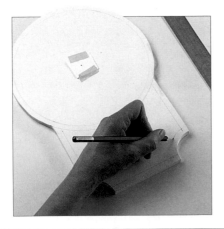

3 Adding the border edges
Continue to draw a ¼ in (6 mm) pencil border around the rest of the clock, using a ruler where necessary.

4 Drawing a border pattern
Draw a freehand pattern of leaves around the border. Use the penciled line as the center of the decorative pattern, with leaves growing from it to the right and left. Continue the border all around the edge of the clock.

TRANSFERRING THE DESIGN

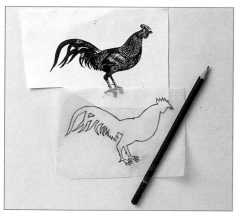

1 **Tracing an image**
Find an image suitable for the lower part of the clock. Here, the image is of a rooster. Trace this image onto a piece of tracing paper.

2 **Transferring the image**
Position the tracing over the clock and tape it down. Slip a piece of transfer/carbon paper underneath the tracing. Then, using a pencil, go over the traced lines to transfer the image onto the clock. Before you remove the transfer/carbon and tracing paper, check to see that you have transferred all the lines.

3 **Transferring clock numbers**
Lay the sheet of clock numbers onto the clock face and secure with masking tape. Slip transfer/carbon paper underneath the sheet, and transfer the clock numbers onto the clock face in the same way as in Step 2. Remove the sheet and the transfer/carbon paper.

Clock-a-Dooddle-Do

As you can see, making this clock — the kind of thing you might expect to find in a French farmhouse — is as easy as 1,2,3. In fact, the only time-consuming task is positioning the numbers evenly.

COLORING THE DESIGN

1 Applying blue lines
Using a fine-tipped blue waterproof marker, go over the lines of the rooster and the clock face numbers on the clock. Then go over all the penciled border lines. Work slowly to avoid smudging the lines and to achieve a crisp, clean effect.

2 Filling in outlines
Carefully fill in the blue outlines with blue acrylic paint using a fine artist's brush and working slowly. Let dry. Erase any remaining pencil marks.

3 Rubbing down
Rub finishing paper lightly over the clock to age and distress the surface, then cover with a coat of acrylic water-based varnish to seal it. When the varnish is dry, insert the clock movement in the central hole, following the manufacturer's instructions.

DESIGN OPTIONS

Fruits of Time
A juicy découpage fruit salad brings a touch of summertime to this clock (below).

Tropical Timepiece
A shoal of exotic painted fish floats across the face of this clock (above) – for the benefit of the innumerate, half past jellyfish is time to make dinner.

Hours Unnumbered
Chunks of colored glass, sandblasted by the ocean and set off by shiny crumpled silver foil, take the place of numbers on this gothic desk-clock face (above).

STENCILED CABINET DOORS

MATERIALS

- Wooden cabinet door
- Wood filler
- Traditional paints: turquoise, lime green, cream, bright blue, orange, sage green
- Matte acrylic water-based varnish
- Masking tape
- Stencil card
- Heavy-duty gloss acrylic varnish

K ITCHEN UNITS ARE A fact of life, and while they draw a discreet veil over the more unattractive aspects of your *batterie de cuisine*, they tend not, in themselves, to conjure up visions of dining beneath a canopy of stars or breakfasting on coffee and croissants while the morning sun slants through a vine-wreathed arbor. However, we have here the recipe for bringing a flavor of Provence to any kitchen business – clever and original citrus stencils in clear, fresh colors that will lift your heart. Give yellowed pine the elbow, and go for exhilarating sky and lagoon blue, orange, terra-cotta, and the soft green of rosemary and sage. It takes courage to use color this pure, but the impact is softened by using two shades of broken, toning background color.

Rubber comb

Sunshine and Citrus

Limes, lemons, and oranges in a carefree composition bring a breath of the south to your kitchen cabinets – a prime example of clever stencil design and shading, with a casual nonchalance rarely found in this technique.

73

PAINTING THE DOOR

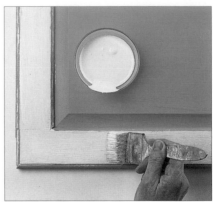

1 Applying the first coat
Fill in any cracks with wood filler and rub it down with sandpaper. Using traditional paint, brush the center panel and the outer edge of the door with a coat of turquoise paint. When dry, paint the frame of the door with a coat of lime green paint and let dry.

2 Varnishing the door
When the surface is dry apply a coat of flat, acrylic water-based varnish over the painted surface of the cupboard door, and let it dry. Use a varnish brush to avoid leaving any obvious brushmarks. This coat of varnish seals the surface and will prevent any spattered paint from soaking into the wood at a later stage of decoration.

3 Painting the frame
When the varnish has dried, paint the frame of the door with cream traditional paint. Apply the paint quickly over the surface with rough brushstrokes. Do not be too concerned about leaving brushmarks since these will be removed when the paint is combed in the next step.

4 Combing the paint
While the paint is still wet, comb it with a rubber comb to create swirly patterns. To do this, hold the comb with two hands and pull it slowly through the paint, applying even pressure on the comb. With a soft cloth, wipe off any paint that spatters onto the edge of the frame. Since the paint is water based it will wipe off easily.

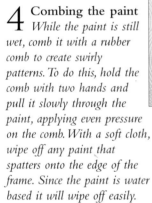

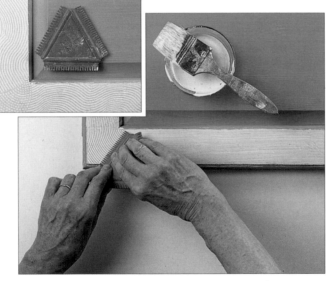

5 Painting the center panel
Mask off the frame's inner edges with masking tape. Apply a coat of bright blue paint over the center panel, brushing it on roughly with a dry paintbrush so patches of the base coat show through. Remove the tape, let it dry, and then varnish.

STENCILING THE DOOR

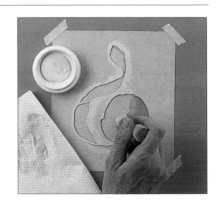

1 Cutting stencils
Draw a simple orange stencil design (see page 217) onto stencil card. Cut out two stencils of the same design with a utility knife. In the first stencil (see Step 2) cut out the whole area of the peeled orange. In the second stencil (see Step 3) cut out the orange segments and only part of the peel.

2 Applying the paint
Position the first stencil on the door and tape it down. Dip a stencil brush in cream paint, dab off the excess on a paper towel, and apply to the stencil. Remove the stencil carefully so as not to smudge the paint.

3 Applying the second color

Place the second stencil over the painted area and tape it down. Dab orange paint through the stencil to create the effect of pitted orange peel. When stenciling the segments, move the brush in a circular motion.

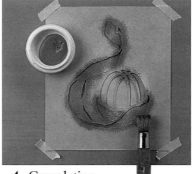

4 Completing the stenciling

Dab sage green paint in the center and edges of the orange to give definition. Stencil the rest of the door using either the same design or adding other stencils – here lemons and limes are added (see page 217).

5 Varnishing the door

Allow the paint to dry, then apply a coat of heavy-duty gloss acrylic varnish for protection. When dry apply a coat of matte acrylic varnish.

DESIGN OPTIONS

Mixed Colors

If you are going to paint a set of matching kitchen cupboards, try out various color combinations on plywood or fiberboard remnants first, to judge the effect. Here (below), terra-cotta was combed with sage green, to interesting effect.

Summer Fruit

All the warmth of summer in one fat melon (above) – the sliced wedge could be extracted as a repeat element and used to embellish curtains. You might even investigate ceramic paints with which to echo the melon theme on fruit bowls and tiles.

Lemon Yellow

Here (above and inset) is the essence of the Mediterranean in one evocative image; it would make a terrific repeat motif running along the bottom of matching blinds. Subtle touches of shading make a huge and three-dimensional difference.

EMBROIDERED SHELF EDGING

MATERIALS

- Interfacing
- Blue water-based paint
- Cardboard
- Sewing thread: green, orange, yellow
- Remnants of colored silk
- Thin ribbon
- Brass tacks

No one would ever pretend that this joyous shelf edging is an essential kitchen accessory, but it does bring a flood of unmitigated cheer to the banal necessity of storage. With its bright, brash Mediterranean colors, a hint of sun and sunflowers, and the simple repeat design, this shelf edging is childishly easy to make and has a quite disproportionate impact. If the spirit moves you, you could apply the same techniques to make a matching finish – using water-based, iron-on fabric paint – for curtains or blinds, or even the hem of a tablecloth. Everyone needs more sunshine in their kitchen.

Flower Border
A sophisticated version of the cutout paper dancing dolls of childhood, this shelf edging brings a touch of sunshine to the most banal pots and jars.

DRAWING OUT AND STITCHING

1 Painting the interfacing
Paint the interfacing with blue water-based paint, daubing the paint on patchily for a textured effect. Allow to dry.

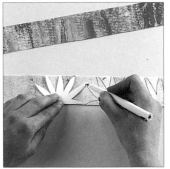

2 Drawing sun outlines
Cut the interfacing into 2 in (5 cm) wide strips, the length of the shelves. Make a cardboard template of half a sun and draw around this along the reverse of each strip, using a fine-tipped marker.

3 Stitching sun outlines
Using a sewing machine stitch along the marked outline using green thread on top and orange thread in the bobbin.

4 Adding appliqué
Cut out several semicircles from colored silk the size of the center of the sun motifs, and several smaller ones in contrasting colored silk. Stitch a large and a small semicircle onto the right side of each sun motif. Using yellow thread, stitch the rays with free stitching (see inset).

FINISHING OFF

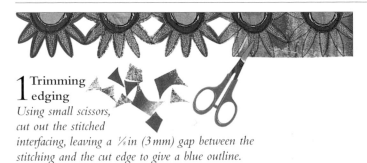

1 Trimming edging
Using small scissors, cut out the stitched interfacing, leaving a ⅛ in (3 mm) gap between the stitching and the cut edge to give a blue outline.

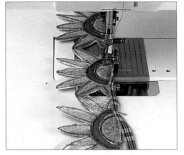

2 Adding ribbon
Fold a thin ribbon over the straight edge of the interfacing to encase it, then pin to secure and stitch it in place with zigzag stitches. Remove the pins. Attach the edging to the shelf using brass tacks placed at intervals along the edging.

PAINTED ACCESSORIES

ACRYLIC WATER–BASED paints have revolutionized the potential of color. They dry in minutes, are nontoxic, cheap, and stable, and are part of an entire decorative system that allows you to be as inventive and experimental as you wish.

To vary the look of a single color you can burnish it with steel wool or use varnishes and glazes to give it a subtle matte or reflective finish. Distressing layers of different color is laughably simple, and stencils, gilding, crackle glaze, or craquelure all add to the repertoire. And the two worst chores in the world, preparation and cleaning up, can be achieved in a matter of minutes, leaving you free to admire your handiwork – and dream up more finishes.

Preparing the surface

You can buy ready-to-paint containers (above), or remove old paint from an existing surface using paint stripper before applying paint.

SQUARED UTENSIL HOLDER

The simplest shape, easily cut by using squared paper as a guide, makes a sophisticated 3-D pattern when repeated off register. If your squares have wavy edges you will achieve a homespun, hand-finished look.

Design Samples

You can vary the look of a simple stencil design such as the arrangements of squares (above), by using different colors and finishes. The top sample was rubbed back with steel wool and sealed with a coat of matte varnish. Parts of the center sample were rubbed with gilt wax, while the bottom one was rubbed back and waxed.

Matte varnish

Sponge

Warm red paint

Dark blue paint

Stencil

Gold paint

Steel wool

Paintbrush

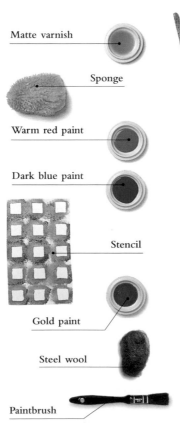

Painting the holder

Paint the box red. Cut your stencil (see page 188). Stencil blue paint on the slightly top left of center on each side with a sponge. When this is dry, stencil gold to the slightly bottom right of center. When dry, rub down with steel wool and seal with matte varnish.

SILVERED CANDLE SCONCE

Silver flame shapes were stenciled onto a dark blue background, and echo the gothic shape of this sconce. The first thing to do is draw the outline of the sconce on paper, mark the position of the shelf, and fit your design into the arch.

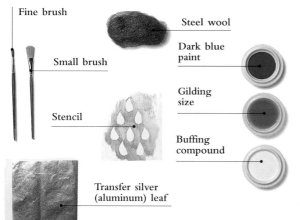

Fine brush

Small brush

Stencil

Steel wool

Dark blue paint

Gilding size

Buffing compound

Transfer silver (aluminum) leaf

Decorating the sconce

Paint the sconce blue. When dry, apply buffing compound and let it dry. Stencil the flames with gilding size (see page 195) using a fine brush, working inward from the cut edge. When this is tacky (in about 5 minutes), rub transfer silver leaf over the stenciled areas with your fingers. The leaf should stick to the sized areas. Remove the backing paper and brush off the excess leaf. Rub back with steel wool and seal with buffing compound.

STENCILED PLANT HOLDER

The motif for this plant pot holder was borrowed from an Indian tobacco box. Draw around one side of the pot and sketch or trace a design *(see page 183)* within that shape. Use a pencil line down the middle to make your design symmetrical. Start with the outline for the pale areas, adding petals wherever you see a space. Fit the green leaves within this outline. Cut a stencil for the cream and one for the green.

Sponge

Steel wool

Light green and dark green mixed paint

Black paint

Terra-cotta paint

Fine brush

Paintbrush

Stencils for cream and green

Matte varnish

Cream and sienna mixed paint

1 Applying first stencil
Paint the cache-pot terra-cotta inside and out. When this is dry, stencil the cream motif on all sides, using the sponge. Let one side dry before tackling the next.

2 Stenciling leaves
Stencil the green leaves roughly in the middle of the cream outline. There is no need to try for perfection. Let this dry. Clean up smudges with a dab of terra-cotta or cream.

3 Adding outline
With a fine brush, outline the larger petals in black, and add a few black whiskers to each. Paint the top edge black. When everything is dry, rub it down with steel wool and seal inside and out with varnish.

IVY WALL SCONCE

The idea here is to match the variegated ivy, and to come up with something suitably ancient-looking to echo the simple gothic sconce. Distressing with a candle is easy and works well on complicated shapes like this. An old nail, dipped in green paint, makes the perfect hanger.

Steel wool

Candle

Paintbrush

Yellow ochre paint

Matte varnish

Raw umber paint

Painting and distressing the sconce
Paint the sconce raw umber. When dry, rub it with a candle and paint it with yellow ochre. Rub back with steel wool, and seal with varnish or wax.

STRIPED UTENSIL HOLDER

This design is taken from an Indian rug woven with uneven spice-bright colors. Irregular stripes are much more interesting than straight lines, and they are very easy to achieve with ripped strips of masking tape, unless you have the courage to paint loose lines freehand.

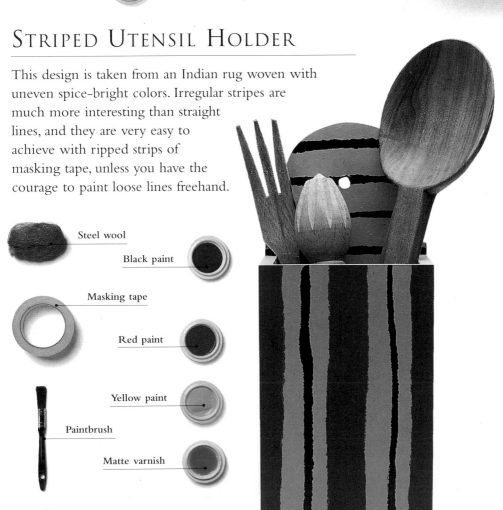

Steel wool

Black paint

Masking tape

Red paint

Yellow paint

Paintbrush

Matte varnish

1 Applying tape
Paint the utensil holder with the base color (yellow) and let it dry. Tear wide masking tape in lengthwise strips – this is not difficult, just take it steady – to stretch from top to bottom of the holder. Position it for a central stripe flanked by two corner stripes on each face of the box, making sure that the rough edges will form the paint guide.

2 Painting stripes
Paint red stripes. Remove the tape. When the red is dry repeat the taping to leave narrow stripes between the red ones and four horizontal stripes at the top. Paint these black. Remove the tape. When dry, rub down with steel wool and seal with varnish.

CRACKLE-GLAZED HOLDER

Crackle glaze has to be one of the most rewarding paint finishes: surprisingly easy to do and extremely impressive. Using gold complicates the procedure – without it you can cut out all the coats of buffing compound.

Crackle glaze

Gilding size

Buffing compound

Dutch metal leaf

Black paint

Dark red paint

Paintbrush

Oil-based varnish

1 Applying the base coat
Paint the candle holder with dark red and, when dry, cover with buffing compound. Leave to dry, then paint the whole surface with gilding size (see page 195).

2 Gilding the holder
When the size is tacky (in about 5 minutes), smooth Dutch metal leaf all over with your fingers. Don't worry too much about gaps and seams, but aim for as complete a coverage as you can manage. Brush off the excess leaf and paint with buffing compound again. Let dry.

3 Applying crackle glaze
Brush on the crackle glaze, in one direction only. When dry, paint the whole thing quickly with black, brushing in the opposite direction. The paint will start cracking, and continue to do so until you add a coat or two of oil-based varnish to seal it.

FORGET-ME-NOT POT

The fresh Mediterranean colors of sea and cloudless skies provide the inspiration for this very easy paint finish. This is so cheap and speedy that you could change the colors to suit your plants – terra-cotta and orange for marigolds, cherry red and green for miniature roses, or slate blue and cream for herbs.

Paintbrush

Candle

Bright blue paint

Green paint

Steel wool

Matte varnish

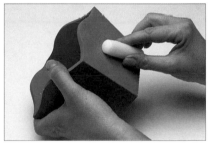

1 Painting and waxing the pot
Paint the cache-pot green inside and out. When dry, buff the inside and rub the outside with a candle to leave an uneven waxy sheen. Paint the outside blue.

2 Rubbing back
When dry, rub the outside with steel wool to reveal patches of the green. Seal with varnish. Use a plastic liner to keep the cache-pot from getting wet.

DÉCOUPAGE BULLETIN BOARD

MATERIALS
- Wine bottles
- Water
- Wooden frame
- White glue
- Hardboard
- Corks
- PVA glue
- Hanging hook

CORK BULLETIN BOARDS are a familiar cliché, relying on the uncomplaining quality of cork to be pinned and pinned again without losing its grip. But there is no regulation stating that the surface has to be flat, and if wine is a favorite beverage, it seems wasteful *not* to recycle all those corks with their attractive stamped legends. The bottle labels, too, evoke hot sunny places and moonlit musings beneath canopied vines. It just seems a pity to obscure the board with anything as banal as bulletins.

COLLECTING LABELS

1 Soaking the labels
Place several empty wine bottles in a bowl of water and leave to soak for 30 minutes. Peel off the wine labels. If they begin to tear, replace the bottles in the water for 15 minutes, then try again. Not every label will come off, so have some spare bottles.

2 Drying the labels
Put the labels aside and leave to dry. You will need enough to cover the frame of the board.

Cork Thoughts
This board (right) exploits the decorative potential of wine corks and labels, while immortalizing fond memories of pleasant evenings. An ordinary junk shop picture frame was the starting point.

ASSEMBLING THE BOARD

1 Applying glue
When the labels are dry, use them to decorate the wooden frame of the bulletin board. First apply white glue to both the frame and the back of each label in turn.

2 Attaching the labels
Stick the labels over the glued frame and smooth them in place with your fingers. Repeat to cover the entire frame with wine labels. Leave to dry.

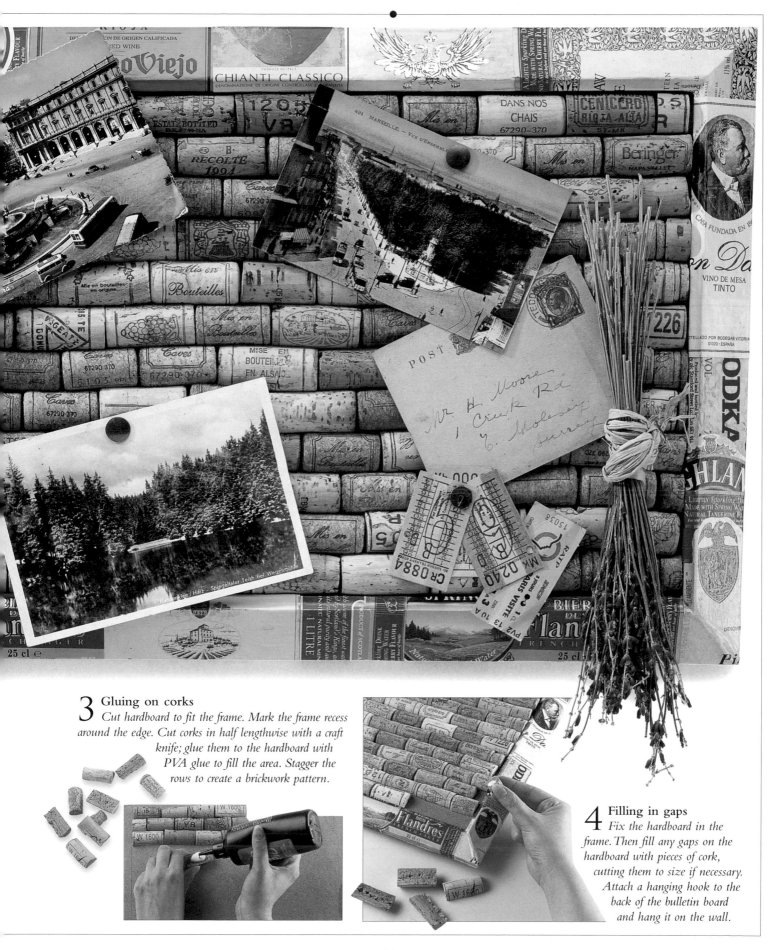

3 Gluing on corks

Cut hardboard to fit the frame. Mark the frame recess around the edge. Cut corks in half lengthwise with a craft knife; glue them to the hardboard with PVA glue to fill the area. Stagger the rows to create a brickwork pattern.

4 Filling in gaps

Fix the hardboard in the frame. Then fill any gaps on the hardboard with pieces of cork, cutting them to size if necessary. Attach a hanging hook to the back of the bulletin board and hang it on the wall.

DECORATED PLANT POTS

MATERIALS

- Terra-cotta plant pots
- White latex paint
- Acrylic water-based varnish
- Masking tape
- Blue pencil
- Blue acrylic paint
- Acrylic water-based glaze
- Paper motif
- Paper glue

THERE ARE FEW domestic sights more depressing than a kitchen windowsill sporting ugly plastic pots containing moldering mint or blighted basil plants. On the other hand, a crisp battalion of terra-cotta painted to match your kitchen, and spilling over with aromatic herbs, is a great incentive to cook with a bit more panache. And if a green thumb eludes you, painted pots make great containers for kitchen paraphernalia. The combination of paint and découpage is easy and effective. The simple expedient of sealing the base coat with acrylic varnish before you attempt anything requiring dexterity makes the entire procedure far less overwhelming since you can rectify any mistakes.

Pot Checks

If you have a sunny kitchen window, you can grow your own parsley, basil, chervil, and cilantro with which to transform your salads. With no sun, you might grow some handsome potted ivy – which will also help to rid your kitchen of chemical vapors, according to a NASA study.

PAINTING THE POT

1 Outlining tape strips
Paint the pot with two coats of white latex paint. When dry, seal with varnish and allow to dry. Stick evenly spaced strips of masking tape vertically down the pot. Using a blue pencil, mark the edges of the tape on the pot. Peel off the tape, then stick strips of tape horizontally around the pot, and outline with pencil.

2 Painting stripes
Mix some blue acrylic paint with a little acrylic scumble glaze (which slows down the drying time of the paint). Using an artist's brush, paint the vertical stripes down the pot, following the penciled lines. Allow to dry, then paint the horizontal stripes in the same way. If you make a mistake, simply wash it off.

ADDING DECORATION

1 Applying a paper cutout
Cut out a paper motif, such as a flower or piece of fruit, from wrapping paper or a magazine. Brush paper glue onto the side of the pot, then stick the motif in position.

2 Sponging off glue
Using a sponge, press the motif into place, easing out any air bubbles and wiping away excess glue. Allow the glue to dry.

3 Varnishing the pot
Varnish the decorated pot with three coats of acrylic water-based varnish, allowing each coat to dry before applying the next.

DÉCOUPAGE TRAY

MATERIALS

- Wooden tray
- Matte black latex paint
- Wrapping paper
- Raw umber paint
- Paper glue
- Gilt cream
- Découpage varnish

A TRAY IS THE PERFECT object for your first foray into découpage. It has a straightforward shape, with an inviting flat surface. Wrapping paper comes in a wonderfully decorative range of designs from which you can cut motifs, or you can plunder seed catalogs and magazines. You can reproduce more precious cards or pictures using a color photocopier. The finished tray can be aged and its design pulled together by using an aging varnish. It is vital to seal a tray completely to keep it clean.

Summer Harvest

This elegant tray is decorated with wrapping paper flowers and fruit, taken from a Dutch still life. Using a dark background confirms the look of an old master, and the gilding around the edge is a refined touch of luxury.

PREPARING THE TRAY

Painting the tray
Apply a layer of matte black latex paint over the surface of the tray using a medium-sized paintbrush. Paint in one direction across the tray. Let dry thoroughly.

PREPARING THE DÉCOUPAGE

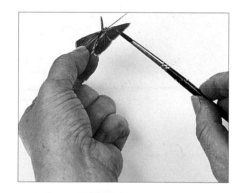

1 Cutting out motifs
Lay your chosen wrapping paper on a flat surface, then cut off the excess parts of your picture with a pair of household scissors. Using small sharp scissors, carefully cut out your motifs (see inset).

2 Painting the cutouts
Using an artist's brush, carefully paint the edges of the cut-out motifs with raw umber paint to ensure that their white edges are not visible.

3 Positioning the motifs
When the cut-out motifs are dry, arrange them on the surface of the tray and move them around, playing with the design of the arrangement until you are satisfied with the overall look.

APPLYING THE PIECES

1 Gluing in place
Glue each large motif separately to the tray by brushing paper glue onto the back of each one and placing it in position on the tray.

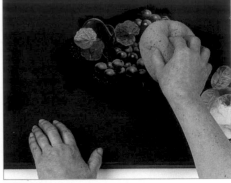

2 Pressing with a sponge
Press each motif gently in position with a damp sponge to ensure there are no air bubbles beneath the paper and that the edges of the paper are glued in place all around.

3 Adding smaller motifs
Glue the smaller motifs in position after you have applied all the larger cutouts. These smaller motifs can be used to fill up any empty spaces.

4 Sponging off glue
Wipe excess glue from the tray using a damp sponge, being careful not to move or tear the paper cutouts. Rinse the sponge several times during this process.

FINISHING THE TRAY

1 Edging with gilt cream
Using your finger, rub some gilt cream along the edges of the tray. Try for a rough "distressed" look, rather than a very hard, solid gold edge.

2 Rubbing with a cloth
When dry, rub down the surface of the tray with a damp cloth to remove any dust particles. This will ensure an absolutely smooth finished surface when the tray is varnished.

3 **Applying varnish**
Paint the tray with a thick layer of découpage varnish, using a varnishing brush to prevent brushmarks from showing. Apply the varnish in one direction.

4 **Rubbing back**
Allow the varnish to dry, then rub the surface gently with fine sandpaper. Wipe with a damp sponge, then with a cloth to remove any dust particles.

5 **Building up layers**
Apply at least five coats of découpage varnish to the tray, sanding and wiping each one in between every couple of coats. If using ordinary varnish, you will need to apply more layers – the more layers you apply, the smoother and more professional the finish will be.

DESIGN OPTIONS

Cherubs and Shells
A pair of pudgy zephyrs and a sprinkling of shells, cut from photocopied engravings and tinted to the rich ocher of ancient vellum, adorn a glossy octagonal tray (right). The fine detail of old steel engravings responds very well to this treatment and confers an impression of hand work without the slightest effort on your part.

Sprigged Circle
A soft green background (below) makes a natural foil to a scattering of summer flowers and butterflies. Small details make a disproportionate difference – a fine gold rim gives this tray a seriously professional air.

Smashing Crockery
Random pictures of tea sets packed in boxes, snipped from wrapping paper, make an apposite decoration for this natural wooden tray (left). Regular repeating motifs look crisp and contemporary.

HOME OFFICE

PAPER-COVERED FILES

MATERIALS
- Box file
- Wrapping paper
- PVA glue
- 8 in (20 cm) length of rope
- Masking tape

EVERYONE HAS DOCUMENTS of one kind or another, but keeping them handy and in good order often seems impossible. Box files are the answer, and if you can make them look good, you may find that efficiency follows. If you have drawers filled with wrapping paper too beautiful to toss, now is the time to recycle it as file covers.

Pressed Flower
A simple daisy glued in place highlights the colors used in the paper covering the file.

Textured Paper
Handmade textured paper adds interesting contrast to a plain-covered file.

Classic Brown Wrap
This version of brown paper is printed with garden tools.

Stenciled Labels
Make stenciled labels for your files (see page 95) to help you keep track of the contents.

Shiny Patches
The unusual Chinese wrapping paper covering this box file is decorated with squares of silver leaf.

Tin Can Ring Pull
This is an inventive answer to a box file necessity — the spine ring pull (see page 94). Be sure that the metal is clean and dry before attaching it to the file.

Decorative Effects
This ornamental box has been decorated with monochrome letters painted on graph paper.

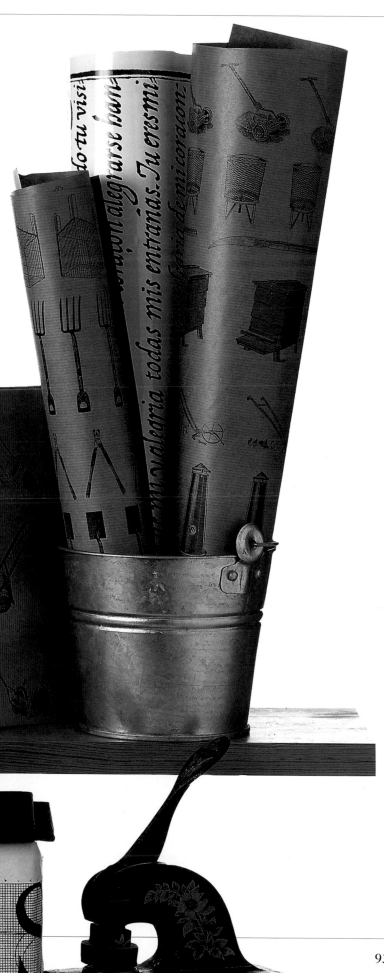

COVERING A FILE

Box files may seem fearsome but they're not high art. You can do anything you like with them; go for an irreverent approach and a neat finish.

Area of box file to be covered

Short sides of box file

1 Cutting out paper covering

Place the open box file on a flat sheet of wrapping paper and draw around the front opening flap (see inset), the spine, the back and the long side edge to make one rectangle, adding on folding flaps. Then draw around the two short sides and add flaps. Cut out the shapes.

2 Gluing sides

Paste the short sides of the box file with PVA glue and stick the paper sides down on the file, right side up. Fold down the flaps and smooth the paper flat.

3 Covering front

Brush glue on the back of the box file and stick the paper in place. Then glue the spine and front of the file and wrap the paper around the file, folding down the flaps around the edges as you go. Leave to dry for at least an hour.

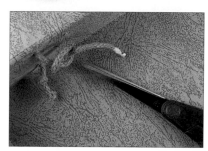

4 Attaching rope handle

Drill two holes in the spine, 4 in (10 cm) from the bottom. Knot one end of the rope; tape the other end. Thread the taped end through the holes and then knot and trim it.

DECORATIVE EXTRAS

ONCE YOU HAVE covered your box file the fun of embellishing it can begin. These pages demonstrate a handful of witty possibilities to make the organization of everyday documents less of a chore. Corners can be made from leather if you are feeling ambitious, or bookbinder's linen. Handles can be shells, fancy nautical knots, shade pulls, corks, clusters of beads, curtain rings, or tiny knobs of glass or brass. Go wherever your imagination leads you: rifle the drawers of hardware stores for interesting tabs, loops, and handles; look anew at the contents of your sewing box for buttons and chunky beads. The object is to be inventive and bring a little charm and humor to your chores. The end result is a creation that looks as mouthwatering as rock candy did when you were six.

Raffia tassel

Black cord tassel

Gold cord tassel

Tassels

Tassels can bring a welcome touch of friskiness to the banal necessity of organizing one's life and, if firmly fixed and sufficiently strong, make convenient handles for grabbing your files. You can buy ready-made tassels in variety or fabric stores, or make your own from embroidery thread, raffia, or fabric strips (see page 41).

• To attach a tassel, thread the ends of the tassel loop through a drilled hole in the spine; stick them down with masking tape or knot firmly in place.

Classy Brass

Drawer knobs and handles are the perfect size for box file spines. Antique metal drawer handles can be found in markets and junk shops. If you buy several, you will be able to decorate an entire shelf of files. Look for matching brass label holders, which you can decorate with calligraphy.

• To attach a drawer handle to a box file, glue a piece of hardboard on the inside of the spine in the position where you want the handle to be attached, then use a screwdriver to screw the handle to the outside of the spine with a screw in each corner.

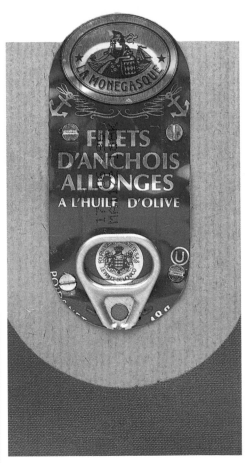

Can Do

Anything that relieves the gloom of dealing with chores is to be welcomed. The decorative potential of tins is miserably underexploited – just take a look at olive oil cans next time you visit a deli.

• Find a tin that still has its ring pull. Wash and dry the tin, then cut out the required shape using metal scissors. Take care, the edges will be sharp. Drill a hole in each corner of the tin and attach it to the file with a screw in each corner.

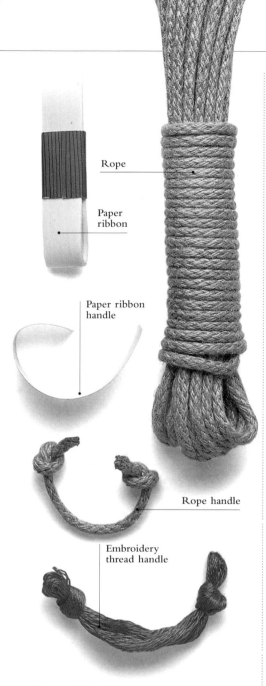

Rope

Paper ribbon

Paper ribbon handle

Rope handle

Embroidery thread handle

Cornered!

Decorate plain box files with colorful corners. In addition to adding decoration, corner pieces protect the file. You can use wrapping paper, waxed paper, or thin cardboard to contrast with or complement the box file. Alternatively, you could use colored bookbinder's linen or even fine leather for a more professional finish.

• To make corner pieces, simply cut out triangles in your chosen material. Trim off the point of each triangle and score along the two short sides to make folding flaps. The flaps should be about ¼ in (6mm) wide. Glue the corner pieces on the front of the box file with PVA glue, and stick the flaps down, holding them in place with butterfly clips until the glue dries.

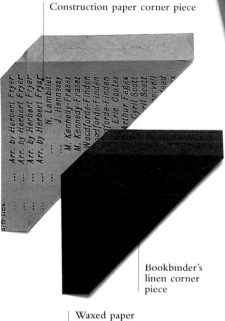

Construction paper corner piece

Bookbinder's linen corner piece

Waxed paper corner piece

Musical score sheet corner piece

Stenciled letter on plain paper

Stenciled letter on plain brown wrapping paper

Loop Handles

A loop handle is a very quick and easy decoration to make for a box file. You can make loop handles from a wide variety of materials. The examples shown above use rope, paper ribbon, and a skein of embroidery thread, but you could use a bunch of fabric strips, colored cord, sisal string, or even small leather straps and thongs.

• Simply drill two holes in the spine of the file, thread the loop handle through the holes, so that the loop is on the outside of the file, and knot both ends on the inside to secure (see step 4, page 93).

Stencils A to Z

Packing-case stencils are clear, punchy, and easy to come by. But you can copy any typeface you like; a different style for every letter of the alphabet could look very smart and graphic.

• Stencils are also extremely easy to make yourself from transparent acetate using a utility knife (with all due caution). If the thought of all this work dismays you, however, its easy to cut out letters from magazines or newspapers and stick them in place. An enlarging photocopier is an adaptable ally for labels with élan. Or you can make a foray into the fine world of calligraphy and practice your italic swashes.

COLLAGE DRAWERS

MATERIALS

- Set of small wooden drawers
- Used stamps
- Terra-cotta latex paint
- Water
- Wallpaper paste
- Gold paint
- Water-based matte varnish

No ONE REACHES adulthood without accumulating a wealth of necessary clutter in the form of paper clips, rubber bands, staplers, pens, and pencils – all the paraphernalia that can never be found when you need it, and requires a baffling struggle with the contents of your desk to retrieve. This enchanting little set of drawers is the answer, although you will then have to struggle with other members of your family who recognize it as just the thing in which to keep makeup, jewelry, nuts and bolts, and all the other small, messy essentials of civilized life. You can safely say that you have put your stamp on this one, but you might be prepared – if everyone is very well behaved and duly grateful – to make one or two others as required.

Stamp Collection

Stamps are not just minor works of art, they also come with memories attached. This colorful collage may well remind you of fond foreign correspondents, and postcards redolent of fun in the sun. If your letters tend to bear only flags waving in the breeze, you could relieve the unalloyed patriotism by using photocopied sections of the letters themselves.

DECORATING THE DRAWERS

1 Soaking the stamps

Soak the stamps in a bowl of water for 2–3 minutes. Then carefully peel them off their envelope backing. Place the wet stamps down flat to dry, glue side facing upward so that they do not stick to the surface.

2 Painting the drawers

Paint the drawers inside and out with a coat of terra-cotta latex paint. When dry, apply a second coat and let dry.

3 Gluing on the stamps

Rub wallpaper paste onto the back of the stamps with your fingers, and place them on the drawers, abutting them tightly to cover the outside of the drawers; leave the drawer knobs, the inside, and the base of the drawers uncovered. Smooth the stamps down to remove any air bubbles. Wipe off excess glue with a soft cloth. Let dry.

4 Painting drawer knobs

Using an artist's brush, paint the drawer knobs with gold paint and allow to dry. Coat the drawers with water-based matte varnish to seal.

DESIGN OPTIONS

Quick on the Draw

A parade of sequins and a decorative button handle would make the perfect drawer front for a jewelry box. A gardener might like storing seed packets in drawers decorated with pressed leaves, and sewing supplies are perfect for storing in drawers edged with tiny mother-of-pearl buttons and opened with a shell.

LAMINATED LAMPSHADE

MATERIALS

- Old lampshade and frame
- Tracing paper
- Handmade paper
- Fusible webbing
- Decorative papers, feathers, etc.
- PVA glue
- Cardboard
- General-purpose adhesive

L AMPSHADES TEND TO BE the poor relations of the design world, yet we all have them, and lighting is the one essential element in any interior. Here is your chance to tackle this neglected opportunity and create a shade that is both attractive and personal.

Having mastered the method, you may want to experiment further to decorate shades large and small. All sorts of things lend themselves to this cunning sleight of light: skeleton leaves, cellophane candy wrappers in stained-glass colors, and postage stamps, for example. For safety's sake be sure there is a gap of at least 1³⁄₁₆ in (3 cm) between bulb and shade, and use a low-wattage bulb – between 25 and 40 watts is ideal.

CUTTING THE DESIGN

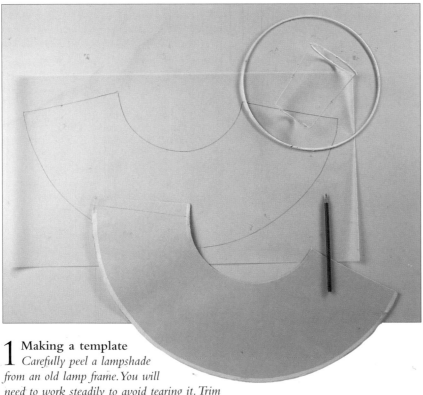

1 Making a template
Carefully peel a lampshade from an old lamp frame. You will need to work steadily to avoid tearing it. Trim the edges if necessary. This shade can then be used as the template for your new lampshade. Place the template down flat on a large piece of tracing paper and, holding it in place with one hand, draw around the edges with a pencil.

2 Sketching the shade design
Cut out the tracing paper shape. On the reverse side of the paper, sketch out the design for the shade with a pencil. You may want to experiment with your design on scrap paper first. Here the shade is divided into five panels; four of the panels feature a simple design, including a star, a feather, and a swirl.

A Light Touch
A cheering light source to leaven the burden of paperwork, this desk lamp is just the sort of dreamy symbol-rich object to get you started on your novel. Experiment with curlicues of cut or torn paper in soft bright colors, scraps of lacy paper doilies, translucent snippets of silk gauze, and dried rose petals to illuminate your desk-bound hours.

DECORATING THE SHADE

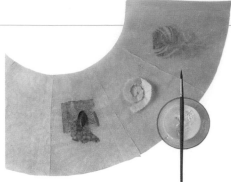

2 Gluing on motifs
Using PVA glue, stick decorative elements such as torn strips and swirls of colored paper on top of the handmade paper panels. Leave two panels undecorated.

3 Pricking patterns
Cut cardboard in the shape of a star. Hold this over the penciled star on the reverse of the shade. Using a stiletto or large needle, poke holes around the outline to create a star pattern of raised dots on the right side of the shade.

1 Laminating decorative motifs
Cut out five panels each of handmade paper and fusible webbing. Lay torn pieces of decorative paper or feathers on two of the marked panels. Iron fusible webbing on top of each marked panel, peel off the backing paper, then iron a panel of handmade paper on each.

ASSEMBLING THE SHADE

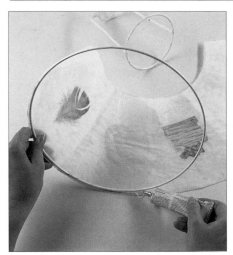

1 Gluing the shade
Using general-purpose adhesive, glue the paper shade to the base of the frame. Apply the glue ⅛ in (3 mm) from the edge of the shade with one hand; hold the frame in place on the shade with the other. When the glue dries, apply another line of glue and roll the frame into it so that the shade sticks to the frame.

2 Completing the assembly
Next, insert the top part of the frame into the shade from the base and glue the edge of the paper to the frame as before. Finally, glue the two edges of the shade together. Leave to dry.

3 Adding paper strips
Using dilute PVA glue, use strips of torn handmade paper to conceal the edges in the paper panels. Pinch the paper between finger and thumb as you stick it down to create added texture.

DESIGN OPTIONS

Literary Lamp

The shade on this slender library lampshade (right) makes much of unprepossessing ingredients. A little imagination is all it takes to dream up something so elegant composed of nothing more opulent than feathers (real and fake) and torn strips of newsprint.

Beachcomber's Lamp

This wire-legged cone (below) is a reminder that storebought lampshades are a snap to customize with sea-booty and other bits and pieces, in this case tiny shells, starfish, ammonite buttons, ocean-tumbled glass, beads, pebbles, and spry copper curlicues. These can easily be stuck in place, or you can dexterously attach them with copper wire, which can look decorative in itself.

Colored Paper Panels

Vary the color of your shade with contrasting paper panels, or add interest to a pale-colored panel with laminated feathery decoration (above).

APPLIQUÉ
ALBUM COVER

MATERIALS

- Assorted pieces of fabric
- Photograph album
- Double-sided tape
- Colored card stock
- Fusible webbing
- Sewing thread

Nicely coordinating fabrics and a simple, bold motif make more impact than the elements would suggest on the countrified cover of this album – the perfect repository for collected birthday cards or wedding congratulations. Naive, Pennsylvania Dutch symbols lend themselves to appliqué, particularly in tiny calico prints, and suggest a garden diary, a house restoration record, successful recipes, or snippets of favorite poetry as contents.

Most people collect memorabilia of some kind, and it is a pity to consign it to dusty oblivion in a bulging shoebox when you could dignify it as an *aide-mémoire* for forays into Sunday-afternoon nostalgia. Try using different fabrics for strikingly different effects; block-printed and striped cottons for a bold look; shiny silks and satins with abstract motifs for something more sophisticated. The secret is to choose closely related, harmonizing fabrics with small patterns, prints, or checks.

A Handy Treasury

No one can resist chunky albums full of memories, and they will eventually become a source of both amusement and fascination to you and your family. It is always a solace to the harassed heart to recall good times, and putting together an album is a serenely therapeutic pastime.

COVERING THE ALBUM

1 Taping the fabric
Cut out a piece of fabric 2 in (5 cm) larger all around than the opened photograph album. Lay the fabric right side down and place the album on the top. Stick strips of double-sided tape around the edges of the inside front and back covers of the album and at the top and bottom of the spine. Fold over the fabric edges onto the tape, mitering the corners, and press down to secure.

2 Covering with card stock
Cut two pieces of colored card stock slightly smaller than the inside front and back covers of the album. Affix double-sided tape to the reverse side of each piece, and stick the card down over the fabric edges on the inside front and back covers.

ASSEMBLING THE DESIGN

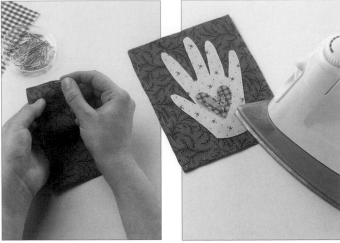

1 Cutting out fabric shapes

Iron fusible webbing onto the reverse of the fabric (see page 38). Cut out all the fabric shapes for your appliqué pattern for the front of the album cover. This simple design is composed of two rectangles, a piece shaped like a hand, and several smaller heart-shaped pieces.

2 Neatening edges

Fold over the edges of the smaller fabric rectangle, press, then pin to retain the crease. Baste the edges. Cut the larger rectangle with pinking shears for a decorative effect.

3 Fusing the motifs

Position the top few layers of appliqué motifs. Remove the backing paper from the webbing, then iron the motifs together. The heat of the iron will melt the glue and fuse the pieces of fabric together.

4 Stitching the heart motifs

Stitch the tiny top heart to the one beneath it using very small catch stitches in matching thread. Then stitch the larger heart to the hand motif beneath it, again using small catch stitches in matching thread.

5 Stitching the hand motif

Using contrasting blue sewing thread, stitch the hand and hearts motif to the small rectangle beneath it, again using very small catch stitches.

6 Adding hearts to the corners

Take four small hearts and position them in the corners of the smaller rectangle. After removing the fusible webbing backing paper from each, iron the motifs so that the glue melts, bonding the fabric together. Stitch each heart in place with a large blue cross stitch in the center. Add a cross stitch in the center of the heart motif on the hand.

7 Blanket stitching

Pin the appliquéd fabric rectangle to the larger fabric rectangle. Stitch in place with blanket stitch around the edges, using cream-colored sewing thread. Remove the basting stitches. Press the appliquéd fabric.

8 Attaching the appliqué

Affix strips of double-sided tape to the edges of the underside of the appliquéd fabric. Position it centrally on the front of the album, then peel off the tape and carefully stick the fabric down.

DESIGN OPTIONS

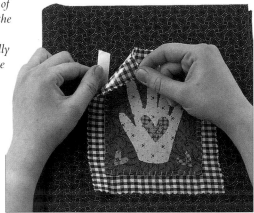

Hearts and Flowers

If a photo album strikes you as too conventional, make motifs to symbolize your garden (left and above), and fill the album with photos, pressed flowers, seed packets, and sketches — or make a Christmas book in berry red and coniferous green to record the festive events of that season.

Home Thoughts

Homemade pieced and patched quilts are a rich source of appliqué motifs, from Sunbonnet Sue to Pennsylvania Dutch tulips, any of which would lend appropriate rustic charm to a scrapbook. This childlike rendition of home (above), lit by a single star, says it all succinctly. Toning checks and gingham with touches of tiny print are crisply harmonious.

GILDED LETTER RACK

MATERIALS

- Wood letter rack kit
- Gold spray paint
- Bronze paint
- Small decorative feathers
- PVA glue
- Cardboard
- Domed upholstery pin

T HE WELL-APPOINTED household has more than one letter rack, since there are myriad other uses for them: to keep cooking notes and recipes tidy and available in the kitchen; to keep receipts safe and orderly in case you have a fit of organization and decide to do your expenses; or to store loose photographs and postcards until those long winter evenings when you have time to arrange them artfully in an album. You could even customize your letter racks for different types of correspondence, using appropriate motifs for "urgent," "reply," "personal," and "bills." The great advantage of letter racks over trays is that they take up a fraction of the space, and you can rifle through the contents easily to judge the scale of the reply operation.

Gold and Feathers
A Midas touch, a well-placed star, and an arrangement of feathers can turn a sensible workaday letter rack into a vision of glamour that might even make a final warning notice lose some of its sting.

PAINTING THE PIECES

1 Spray painting
Lay the dividers and base of the letter rack kit on spare paper to protect your surface. Spray both sides of the components with gold paint and let dry.

2 Painting details
Using an artist's brush, paint the molded details of the letter rack divider with bronze paint. Let dry.

ASSEMBLING THE LETTER RACK

1 Decorating with feathers
Arrange feathers in a semicircular fan-shape on the front divider. When satisfied with their position, apply PVA glue along the bottom third of each feather's spine and stick in position. Let dry.

2 Cutting out a star
Draw a star shape on cardboard. Cut it out using a craft knife. Spray this star with gold paint and let dry.

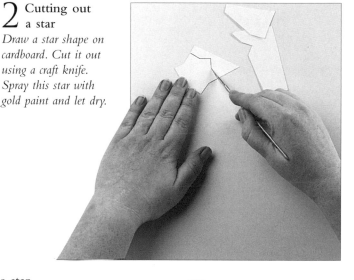

3 Attaching the star
Insert a domed upholstery pin through the center of the gold star; mark the center point of the front divider. Line up the pin with the marked point and hammer it through gently, holding a piece of cardboard between the hammer and the pin to prevent the pin from being dented. Hammer the pointed end of the drawing pin downward on the reverse of the divider to secure.

4 Assembling the pieces
Assemble the letter rack by gluing the separate elements together with PVA glue. Let dry.

STAMPED PICTURE FRAME

MATERIALS
- Wooden frame
- Latex paint: terra-cotta, black
- Tissue paper
- Gold acrylic paint
- Printing stamp
- Fine lining/masking tape
- Acrylic water-based varnish

CUSTOMIZING PICTURE FRAMES is the quickest, speediest, and most rewarding of home projects. You can play with the entire decorative spectrum of techniques, from simply stamping a design on a frottaged background as here, to splattering, sponging, gilding, découpage, and even craquelure or crackle-glazing. In this project we have used a ready-made stamp, but it is also very easy to design your own and cut it out in cork (*see page 111*).

Fine Feathers
Frame and picture should be mutually enhancing – you could not do much better than this engraved peacock bordered by golden feathers.

PREPARING THE FRAME

1 Sanding the frame
Wrap a piece of sandpaper around a block and rub this over the frame. This roughens the wood to give a key to the surface, making it ideal to paint.

2 Painting the frame
Paint the front, and inner and outer sides of the frame with a coat of terra-cotta latex paint. Let dry.

3 Applying a second color
Mix a little black latex paint into the terra-cotta paint, then brush this over the front and sides of the frame.

4 Frottaging the frame
While the paint is still wet, frottage the surface by laying a piece of tissue paper over the frame, then carefully lifting it off. The tissue will create a subtle pattern, rather like leather, on the surface of the frame. Allow to dry.

STAMPING THE FRAME

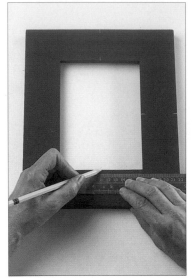

1 Marking the center
Using a ruler and pencil, mark the midpoint of each side of the frame. This will allow you to position the stamp accurately on each side of the mark.

2 Inking the stamp
Using a paint roller and gold acrylic paint, ink the printing stamp. Do not put too much paint on the stamp or the print will smudge.

3 Printing the motifs
Align the edge of the stamp with the penciled point on one side of the frame and lay it on the surface, pressing down firmly. Then lift up the stamp to reveal the printed motif. Continue to stamp motifs around the frame, rolling on more paint as and when it is required. Allow to dry.

COMPLETING THE DECORATION

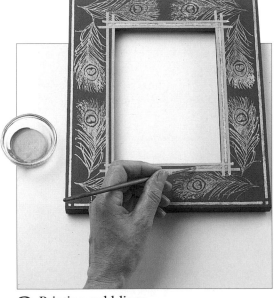

1 Masking edges
Mask off a thin line around the inner and outer edges of the frame. To do this, apply three adjacent strips of fine lining or masking tape along each edge. Peel off the middle strip in each case.

2 Painting gold lines
Paint the thin masked lines with gold acrylic paint using a fine artist's brush. When you have finished painting, peel away the rest of the fine lining or masking tape. Allow the paint to dry.

3 Varnishing the frame
Apply a coat of acrylic water-based varnish all over the frame to seal it, and let dry.

MAKING A STAMP

1 **Drawing and cutting out**
Draw a decorative motif on a cork tile using a black felt-tip pen. Carefully cut out the motif with a craft knife.

2 **Attaching the block**
To make the stamping block, attach the cork motif to a small block of wood using PVA glue. Let dry.

DESIGN OPTIONS

Gold Stars
This Chinese red is brought to life by random gold stars, some dense and some more ethereal, printed with a ready-made star shape (right).

Gilded Tiles
Here a ready-made rubber stamp with a crisp tile design is printed with gold over cream latex (below).

Cinnabar Pinwheels
These vigorous spinning devices were traced onto cork, cut carefully with a craft knife, and printed in foxy red onto yellow (above).

Green Flowers
A speckled veil of color is conferred by a ready-made foam shape printed in green on russet (left).

DÉCOUPAGE WASTEPAPER BASKET

MATERIALS

• Wooden wastepaper basket
• Terra-cotta latex paint
• PVA glue
• Candy wrappers
• Water-based matte varnish

A GLAMOROUS TRIBUTE TO AN expanding waistline, this elegant wastepaper basket is decked with a decadent flurry of shimmering candy wrappers. Never have so many calories been used to such decorative effect! More cautious eaters could make a less wicked basket using comic strips, used stamps, découpaged roses cut from a nursery catalog, overlapping layers of tissue paper, or patchwork squares of wrapping paper. Whatever you choose, try to use colors that harmonize, and paint the whole thing with a complementary base coat before you begin. Metallic papers, as used here, can be given a smooth sheen by burnishing with the back of a spoon.

DECORATING THE BIN

1 Painting the surface
Paint the inside and the lip of the wastepaper basket with two coats of terra-cotta latex paint, allowing the first coat to dry before applying the second. When dry, apply a coat of PVA glue over the painted surface to seal.

2 Gluing on wrappers
Collect an assortment of candy wrappers in complementary colors. Here, the colors are browns, golds, and reds. Smooth them out carefully so as not to tear the paper. Brush PVA glue on the unpainted sides of the wastepaper basket, a small area at a time, then glue down the candy wrappers. Abut them tightly to cover the outside of the basket completely. Let dry.

3 Burnishing
Gently burnish the wrappers using the back of a spoon. This brings out the shine of the papers and removes any air bubbles. Then apply a coat of water-based matte varnish over the entire surface to seal.

Bin There, Done That

A flurry of autumnal browns and golds
recycled from an orgy of chocoholic excess
turns a simple wastepaper basket
into a gleaming receptacle fit for
the most select trash.

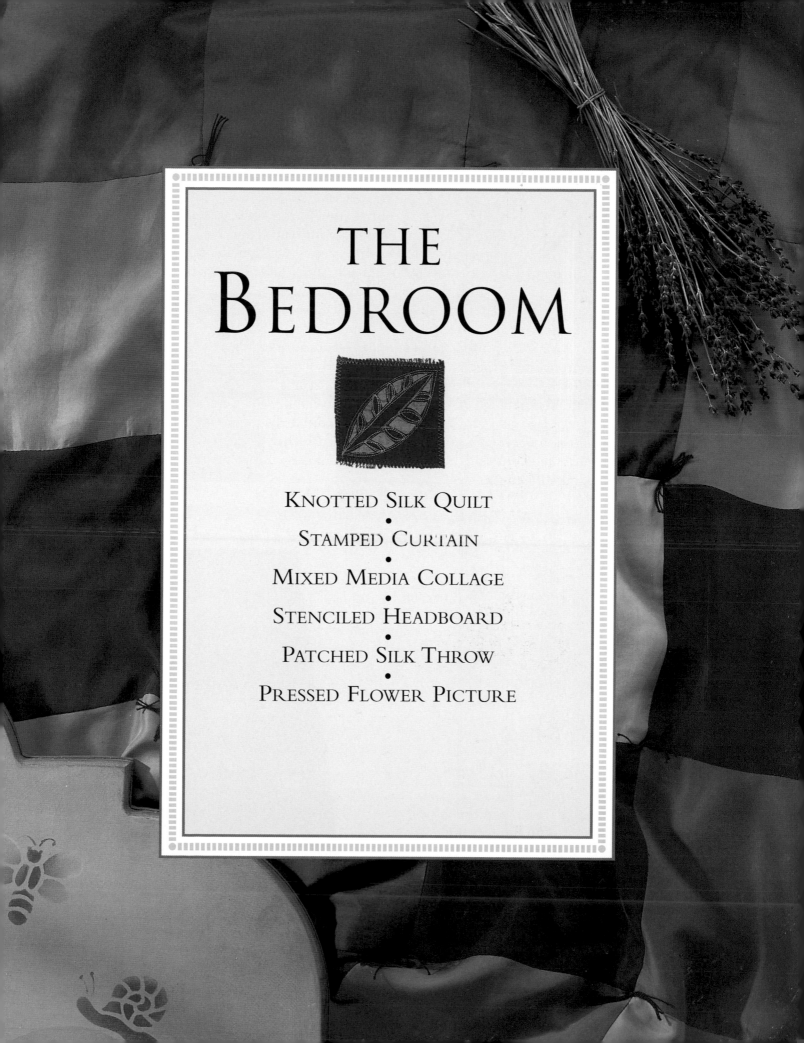

THE
BEDROOM

Knotted Silk Quilt

•

Stamped Curtain

•

Mixed Media Collage

•

Stenciled Headboard

•

Patched Silk Throw

•

Pressed Flower Picture

KNOTTED SILK QUILT

MATERIALS

- Cardboard
- Old silk shirts: enough for 40 9¼ in (23 cm) squares
- Silk thread
- 56 x 80 in (140 x 200 cm) calico for backing
- 56 x 80 in (140 x 200 cm) batting
- Perlé thread

N O ONE WOULD PRETEND that silk, the unsurpassed queen of textiles, is appropriate for hard usage, but it is surprisingly hardwearing, washes without demur (all these patches came from old silk shirts and have seen the inside of a washing machine many a time), and is absolutely impossible to beat for refined, glowing color and irresistible texture.

As a matter of banal practicality, knotting is an incredibly speedy and stylish way of holding the three layers of the quilt sandwich in place; it is entirely successful when the interlining (batting) is woven, rather than the traditional filling of loose sheeps' wool, which had to be minutely stitched into place with intricate quilted patterns.

Quick Quilting

Tie quilting knots in different-colored embroidery threads for a contrast in both color and texture.

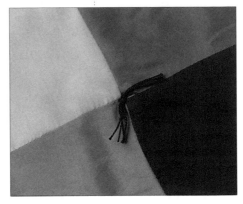

MAKING THE QUILT

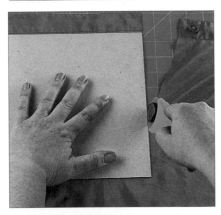

1 Cutting out
Make a cardboard template measuring 9¼ x 9¼ in (23 x 23 cm). Place this on the silk and, using a rotary cutter for speed and protecting your surface with a cutting mat, cut out 40 squares.

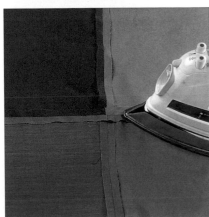

2 Joining squares
Leaving a ⅝ in (1.5 cm) seam, stitch the silk squares together in eight rows of five squares, varying the colors. Press the seams open at the end of each row. Place the rows side by side and stitch together, leaving a ⅝ in (1.5 cm) seam allowance. Press the seams open.

3 Adding the border
Cut out four strips of silk for the border 8 in (20 cm) wide; two strips should equal the long side of the pieced rows, two strips should equal the short side plus 16 in (40 cm). Stitch the two border strips to the long sides of the quilt, right sides facing and matching raw edges. Then stitch the two shorter sides of the border to the quilt. Press all seams open.

FINISHING OFF

1 Making binding
Cut four strips of silk 3¼ in (8cm) wide and equal to the lengths of the long and short sides of the quilt plus ¾ in (2cm). Iron each strip in half lengthwise, then open out the strip and iron both long edges into the center. Iron under ⅜ in (1cm) on each short end.

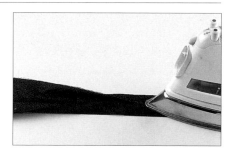

2 Assembling quilt layers
Lay the calico backing down flat. Place the batting on top, then lay the quilt on top of that and pin the three layers together. Machine stitch through the three layers around the four edges. Remove the pins. Fold the binding over the edges. Pin, then topstitch through all the layers. Remove the pins.

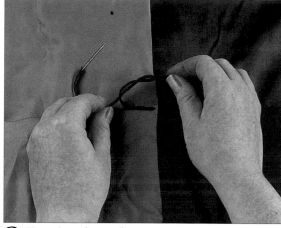

3 Knotting the quilt
Using a large-eyed crewel needle and two strands of perlé thread, make knots at the corners of the squares. Insert the needle through the quilt from front to back and then bring it out to the front again at the side of the needle's first entry, keeping the ends of the thread at the front. Tie a reef knot with the thread ends, then trim the ends.

Opulent Patches

This sumptuous quilt is a magnificent final destination for a wardrobe of silk shirts whose excessive shoulder pads or frayed cuffs have relegated them to the scrapbag.

DECORATIVE EXTRAS

As A GLANCE THROUGH any American decorating book will show, there are as many styles of quilts as there are stitchers to sew them – you can be as countrified as a cornfield, or as chic and sophisticated as a space-age kettle, as innocent as a daisy or as complex as a combustion engine, and there will be an embarrassment of quilt designs to match your mood. You do not even need to explore the intricacies of piecing or stitching: the fabrics alone, put together in basic squares, give the finished quilt its

character. Here is a dazzling array of scrapbag plunder, all making use of the same simple technique of machine-stitched squares and knotting in place of quilting.

Now that it is no longer necessary to stitch the quilt minutely all over, there is the glorious time-saving possibility of using evenly spaced knots to hold the sandwich together. The only essential is to stretch the whole quilt out taut and flat in order to pin through the layers before you start to knot.

Sentimental Squares

These squares of linen in interestingly offbeat colors are embellished with two of the all-time favorite appliqué motifs for quilts and covers: hearts and flowers, neither of which ever fails to arouse a friendly response, and both of which are easy to draw. Here, the designs have the sweet naïveté of a child's drawing, an impression that is reinforced by the use of gingham and big stitches. But a sophisticated palette of acid green, slate blue, and terra-cotta tends not to feature among the fingerpaints.

• *To decorate with appliquéd motifs, iron a piece of fusible webbing onto the appliqué fabric. Then draw a simple motif on the fusible webbing and cut out the shape. To secure the motif to the fabric, iron the fusible webbing again, which will melt the glue, peel off the fusible webbing paper backing, and stick the motif down onto the quilt square, glue side down. Secure the motif in place with stitches, using a contrasting-color thread for interest.*

Chintz and Checks

Mixing woven checks and prints successfully is a matter of balance and careful color matching. Here the pinky beige and maroon of the check precisely match the honeysuckle, a skillful bit of visual analysis picked up by the dark knotting. The two patterns combine very effectively, with wild and formal elements in mutually flattering counterpoint.

• *When choosing fabrics to use together on your quilt, look for an element that links them. Spots work well with stripes, for example, if they are the same color or shade of color. Likewise, flowery fabrics work well with plain if there is a color match with one of the flowers. The fabrics themselves should also be compatible; use either all silks, or all cottons, not mixtures of the two, or you might ruin your quilt in the washing machine.*

Sunburst Silks

A common denominator of sunshine yellow links these cheery checked and striped squares of silk, knotted with a matching chunky tassel, which has been very neatly trimmed. Tassels like this can be a telling element in themselves, and can contrast, in terms of both color and fiber, using multicolored strands of silk, or wool teased out. Alternatively, you can sew buttons, beads, or even sequins to hold the batting in place, make tiny tufted pompoms, or keep the knotting discreetly hidden on the back of the quilt.

• *To make a tassel from embroidery thread to match the quilt, cut ten pieces of thread, 6 in (15 cm) long. Fold the bunch of thread in half and tie another piece of thread tightly around the bunch, about one third of the way along the bunch from the fold. Stitch the tassel to the quilt, taking the stitches through all the layers of the quilt to secure.*

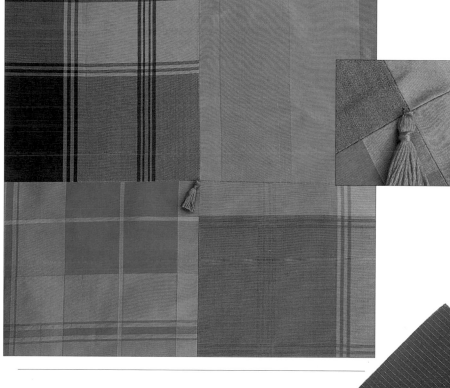

Scarlet and Black

A virtuoso exercise in piecing and stitching, this artistic abstraction in striped denim works so well because the stripes are perfectly matched. If you are going to do this kind of thing, which is very easy and blindingly effective, you must be prepared to work hard – possibly to the extent of pinning and basting – to get the stripes to meet exactly. It is an annoying rule in life that the more spectacular the ambition, the more exasperating the failure. If your stripes miss each other, that is what your eye will be inexorably drawn to.

• *To match stripes between patches, place one patch on top of another, with right sides together, and align the stripes by eye. Then pin along the adjoining edge, turn the patches the right way up, and check that the stripes match. If not, readjust accordingly. Repeat this process when joining all the patches. You may also want to baste the patches before stitching.*

Indigo Pinstripes

Woven patterns of just two colors have a very crisp executive look about them. The important thing to aim for is an even balance of tones – here the two dark and the two lighter squares are perfectly balanced. Over an entire quilt, the eye is very quick to be irritated by a stray light or dark patch. Dealing with woven patterns also requires accurate stitching along the stripes.

• *To ensure you have an even balance of tones in your quilt, lay out all the patches in the desired design before you begin to stitch, so that you can rearrange their order if necessary.*

STAMPED CURTAIN

MATERIALS

- Paper
- Cardboard
- PVA glue
- Block of wood
- Fabric paints
- Plain muslin or cotton curtain

FABRIC PRINTING DOES NOT have to be complicated to be effective. This curtain is simply stamped with a cardboard stamp cut in the shape of a fleur-de-lis, in two colors on plain muslin. The result is clean, stylish, and modern. A crisp repeating design like this, applied with easily available fabric paint that can be fixed with an iron, makes customized furnishings a possibility for everyone. Muslin is a good starting point, because it is cheap and has a pleasant character of its own. You need not fear making the odd mistake with a fabric that costs the same per yard as a cup of coffee. The one drawback is that it does tend to shrink, so you would be wise to prewash it, which unfortunately implies hours of patient ironing.

MAKING AND USING THE STAMP

1 Cutting out motifs
Draw a simple fleur-de-lis shape onto a piece of paper. This will be your stamping motif. Cut it out carefully, then draw around the shape twice onto thick cardboard. Cut out the two identical motifs with a craft knife. Repeat this process to make a simple border motif.

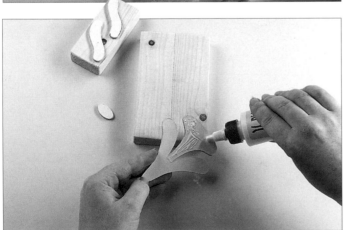

2 Making the blocks
Using PVA glue, stick the two identical cardboard shapes together for each motif. Then glue each motif to a separate small block of wood to create stamping blocks.

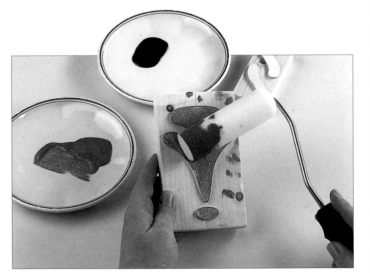

3 Inking up the block
Pour some fabric paint into a saucer. Using a foam paint roller, apply paint to the stamping block; too much paint might cause the print to smudge. Do a few trial prints before stamping the curtain.

Calico Swags

Simple stamps are not difficult to make, and you can use them to print fabric in a spare and elegant style, or use bright colors, irregular placing, and overprinting if you favor something slightly more hectic. In the wake of Walt Disney, you might be able to persuade your dog to run over an ink pad, and then tap-dance on your fabric. Alternatively, you might just make a witty stampable version of animal paw prints with which to print your curtains.

4 Stamping the pattern
Lay the calico curtain on a work surface and press the stamping block evenly on the fabric. Lift up the block carefully to reveal the stamped motif. Repeat to decorate the entire curtain, inking up the block for every print.

5 Stamping the border
Stamp a second motif around the edges of the curtain in a contrasting color, ensuring that you align the stamping block each time. When you have completed the printing, allow the fabric paint to dry, then iron the reverse side of the fabric with a hot iron to fix the paints.

MIXED MEDIA COLLAGE

MATERIALS
- Paper
- Gesso
- Water
- PVA glue
- Silver wrapping paper
- Gauze
- Blue and pink embroidery floss
- Colored paper
- Lavender stems and heads
- Blue wax crayon
- Mounting board
- Frame

EVERYONE STRIVES TO be efficient and businesslike, but it is good to recall from time to time that sentiment and nostalgia are not against the law. This collage is a very pretty object in its own right, but its cargo of hearts suggests a Valentine or anniversary present, so celebrate your passions, and wear your heart on your wall. The delicate colors, layers of gilding, and soft translucent fabric are utterly feminine, paying charming homage to a quaint, old-fashioned concept that still satisfies some, no doubt politically very incorrect, primeval urge. This collage draws on an interesting variety of techniques, which would lend themselves happily to showing off almost any collection of memorabilia.

CREATING TEXTURE

1 Applying the gesso
Sketch a simple design. Here the design is of squares and hearts. Tear a square of paper for the background. Mix together 2 tablespoons of gesso, 3 teaspoons of water, and 1 teaspoon of PVA glue. Add more water if necessary until the mixture is the consistency of heavy cream. Paint the gesso mixture onto the center of the paper. Move it around with the brush to form lumps and ridges. Allow to dry for at least two hours.

2 Decorating with silver paper
Cut silver wrapping paper into squares. Paste PVA glue onto the reverse of each paper square in turn, and then stick it on the dried gesso. Press the paper with a finger to mold it into the shape of the dry gesso.

COMPLETING THE COLLAGE

1 Stitching gauze squares
Cut out squares of translucent gauze and fray the edges. Using embroidery floss, stitch the squares to the left side of the collage and across the bottom with running stitches around the edges of each square.

2 Gluing paper squares and stitching a heart
Glue small squares of colored paper to the lower right side of the collage, cutting a heart shape out of one of them. Draw a heart on the right side of the collage in pencil. Using pink embroidery floss, stitch rows of straight stitch in the area around the heart so that the heart appears in relief.

3 **Adding lavender**
Stitch gauze squares to the right of the collage. Glue a paper heart to a gauze square at the base. Stitch lavender stems to the base. Then dab vertical rows of PVA glue on to one gauze square and place single lavender heads on the glue with tweezers. Allow to dry.

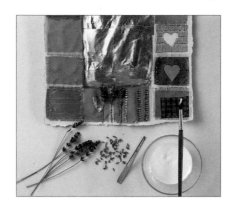

4 **Drawing a heart**
Using a blue wax crayon, draw a heart on the central silver section. Smudge it with a finger to make a blurred heart shape. Glue the finished collage onto mounting board and fix in a frame to hang on the wall.

Lavender's Blue
Muted, misty colors give this collage (above and right) *a peaceful presence – just the thing to soothe fretful spirits, and remind you that there is life beyond noise and haste.*

STENCILED HEADBOARD

MATERIALS

- Wooden headboard
- Traditional paint in muted tapestry colors
- Water-based acrylic varnish
- Stencils *(see page 218)*
- Masking tape
- Matte acrylic varnish

THIS IS A HEADBOARD guaranteed to ensure life-enhancing dreams, with its enchanting images of butterflies, vines, and cherry-picking bluebirds. Stencils will always be the most brilliant method of reproducing a design. They do not have the hard, overworked edge of nervous freehand painting, but the real skill lies in giving the paint shade and subtlety. To my mind, a small natural sponge is more controllable and gives a more interesting stipple than a stencil brush. But the discovery of favorite tools and infallible methods, however quirky and personal, is a large part of the pleasure of making things.

PAINTING THE HEADBOARD

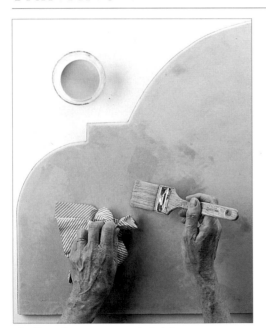

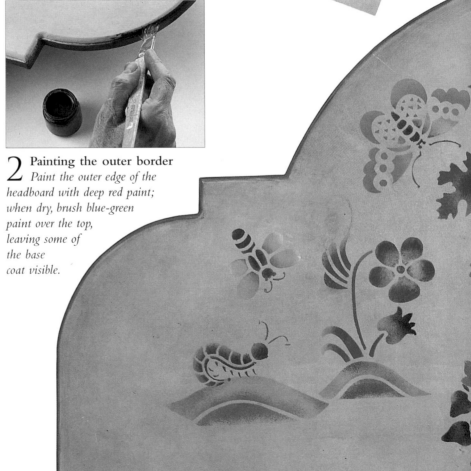

2 Painting the outer border
Paint the outer edge of the headboard with deep red paint; when dry, brush blue-green paint over the top, leaving some of the base coat visible.

1 Creating a textured finish
Sand the edges of the headboard. Apply a coat of putty-colored paint; when dry, seal the surface with varnish. Then apply diluted ocher paint; dab this with a crumpled soft cloth to create texture. Varnish to seal.

STENCILING THE HEADBOARD

1 Dabbing on paint
Position the tree and bird stencil (see page 218) in the center of the headboard; secure with masking tape. Using a stenciling brush, dab green and brown paint over the stencil, overlapping the color, and emphasizing edges to give depth.

2 Adding more color
Carefully position the bird section of the stencil and stipple on more colors, here deep red and light blue, overlapping the colors slightly to avoid any hard edges.

3 Stenciling additional motifs
Continue to add more elements of the design until you are satisfied with the result. This butterfly design is stenciled in blues and browns.

4 Softening the stenciling
When you have finished stenciling, allow the paint to dry. Then apply a coat of diluted blue paint over the surface, and dab this quickly with a crumpled cloth to soften the stenciling. Let dry, and then apply a coat of flat acrylic varnish to seal. Let it dry.

Dream Garden

A quirky assemblage of flora and fauna, with a slightly medieval air (left), is very likely to sweeten slumbers with charming botanical reveries.

PATCHED SILK THROW

MATERIALS

- Colored silk:
25 12in (30cm) squares
25 7in (17.5cm) squares
- Multicolored rayon thread
- Green rayon thread
- Cotton polyester thread
- Decorative buttons
- Lining fabric

A COLLECTION OF HANDSOME THROWS is an essential interior design resource. A new throw is an instant change of character, a source of good cheer, a splash of light or bright color in a quiet scheme of neutrals, and, in some cases, a valuable answer to winter's chill. This splendid example is in the dramatic vein, all rich, sumptuous color and texture, exploiting the natural ability of raw silk to absorb dye and reflect light. The bold reverse appliqué design is simple to achieve and the zigzag stitching that holds the motifs in place is both quick to do and a decorative element in itself. It is worth pointing out that silk is astonishingly inexpensive today, particularly as remnants in large fabric shops.

Leaf Throw

A reinterpretation of patchwork, this bold silk throw with its reverse appliqué leaves is rich with resonant color. Use it to add an effortless dash of style and drama to a cozy couch or a wan windowseat.

MAKING THE SQUARE PATCHES

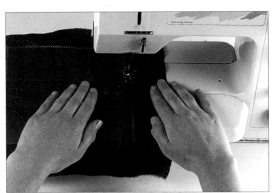

1 Preparing the squares
Cut out 25 silk squares measuring 12in (30cm) and 25 measuring 7in (17.5cm). Using multicolored rayon thread, zigzag stitch a small square to the center of each large square around its edges.

2 Marking a design
Using tailor's chalk, mark a simple leaf design on each central silk square. For reference and inspiration, look at books on gardening or simply trace a motif from page 129 and enlarge it on a photocopier to the required size.

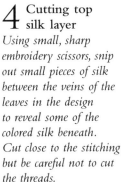

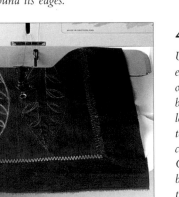

3 Stitching the design
Attach the darning foot on the sewing machine and drop the feed dog. Then, using green rayon thread, stitch along the chalked lines with straight stitching.

4 Cutting top silk layer
Using small, sharp embroidery scissors, snip out small pieces of silk between the veins of the leaves in the design to reveal some of the colored silk beneath. Cut close to the stitching but be careful not to cut the threads.

ATTACHING PATCHED STRIPS

COMPLETING THE THROW

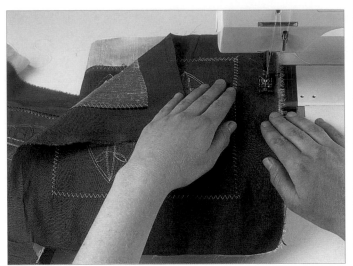

1 Joining squares
Using the presser foot on the machine and with the feed dog up, stitch two squares together using cotton polyester thread. Place the squares together, right sides facing, and stitch along the edge, using a ⅝ in (1.5 cm) seam. Repeat to make a strip of five squares. Then repeat to make four more strips with five squares in each strip.

1 Adding buttons
Using colored cotton polyester thread, hand stitch decorative buttons onto the front of the throw at the junctions of all the large silk squares.

2 Attaching backing
Cut out lining fabric the same size as the throw. Pin this to the throw, right sides facing. Stitch around all four sides, leaving a 6 in (15 cm) gap on one side. Turn the throw right side out through the gap.

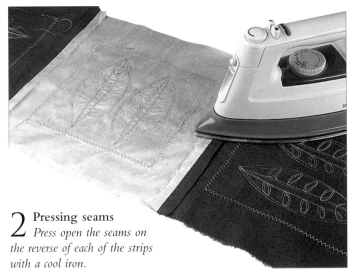

2 Pressing seams
Press open the seams on the reverse of each of the strips with a cool iron.

3 Joining the strips
Stitch all the strips together, again using a ⅝ in (1.5 cm) seam down the long side of each strip. Turn the fabric over and press all the seams open. You should now have a square throw consisting of 25 squares – five squares wide and five squares long.

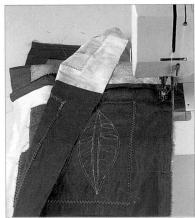

3 Slipstitching
Pin, then slipstitch the gap in the throw to close, using cotton polyester thread. Press the throw before using.

DESIGN OPTIONS

Jungle Colors

Splashy green and magenta shot silk leaves, as long as jungle bromeliads and arranged side by side as positive and negative, make a dramatic design. This would be a stunning cushion cover, but it is too powerful to cover a large expanse.

Leaf Quartet

Strong, vibrant tones, enlivened by a flash of checks, produce a random kaleidoscope of color. This flurry of multicolored leaves is held together with a formal and disciplined layout; each one is clearly outlined in contrasting thread, and they are laid out in a circle, a comforting and contained shape.

PRESSED FLOWER PICTURE

MATERIALS

- Flowers and leaves
- 2 sheets of blotting paper
- Mounting board
- Watercolor paper
- Contact adhesive
- Dark green watercolor paint
- Frame

A PICTURE OF INNOCENCE, this collection of pansies, violets, honesty, pelargoniums, and lavender, with the odd sprig of foliage, expresses the whole of summer in a small space. A charming and nostalgic exercise, pressing and arranging flowers produces a touching *aide-mémoire* that will remind you of a particular glorious summer whenever you look at it. Details count for a lot – the tiny flowers outlining the Romanesque mount give a traditional air to the ensemble, and the formality of the design removes any tendency to over-sentimentality.

Summer Sprigs

A garden in summer is a bountiful source of shapes and colors – pansies with their streaked "faces," glistening rose petals and buttercups, and bright pelargoniums are just a few of the possibilities. Fern fronds have a lacy delicacy, while anemone petals contribute rich, satiny color.

Billet-Doux

Spring flowers massed on cardboard or heavy paper make a memorable Easter greeting – here is an unforgettable bouquet of pansies, primroses, auriculas, and clematis.

PRESSING THE FLOWERS

1 Preparing the flowers
Remove petals from bulky flowerheads such as roses and press them separately. Thin out multipetaled flowers by snipping off some petals.

2 Positioning flowers
Using tweezers, carefully place the flower material on a sheet of blotting paper. Leave a space between each flower and leaf to allow for them spreading when pressed. Ensure the flower material is of a similar thickness for even pressing.

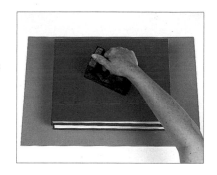

3 Covering with blotting paper
Place another sheet of blotting paper on top of the flower material to cover it completely. This will absorb any moisture from the flowers when they are pressed.

4 Applying pressure
Place a couple of heavy books on top of the blotting paper, then place a weight on top of these. Leave for six to eight weeks, by which time the flowers will be dried and thoroughly pressed, and ready to be used.

MAKING THE PICTURE

1 Cutting a mount
Place a rectangle of mounting board on a cutting mat, and draw an arch-shaped frame in pencil on it. Then, using a craft knife, cut out the frame, working carefully so as not to tear the mounting board and to ensure a neat edge.

3 Building up the flower picture
Once the border is complete, glue the central elements of the picture in position. To create a sampler effect, work in rows, placing small flowers at the top of the picture and larger flowers toward the bottom.

2 Gluing the border
Place the cutout frame over a rectangle of paper to mark the picture area. Begin to glue the pressed flowers and leaves onto the paper, starting with the border. Hold the flowers with tweezers, and dab glue onto each flower with a toothpick.

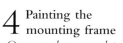

4 Painting the mounting frame
Once you have completed the flower picture, remove the mounting board frame and paint it with one coat of dark green paint to complement the color of the flowers. Let dry, then glue in position around the picture. Complete the picture with a frame of your choice.

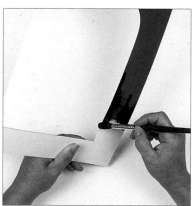

THE
BATHROOM

DECORATED GLASS BOTTLES

MATERIALS
- Glass bottle and stopper
- Turpentine
- Glass paint
- Outline relief paste

RICH, TRANSLUCENT COLORS – bright blue and ruby red, with a filigree of festive gold – make transforming plain glass bottles into Renaissance treasures as easy as painting by numbers. Simple and delicate patterns of dots and stripes, stars and hearts, flowers and leaves are all done in a matter of moments and give clear glass the dazzle of Aladdin's cave. Pretty perfume bottles and jars are often among the inexpensive booty to be found in antique shops. Using the same technique, you can decorate humble drinking glasses and jars to make jewel-like votive lights for your table, or for twilight dining in the garden. Or you can embellish bowls and vases, and tackle glazed door panels with the stained-glass colors of a Gothic cathedral.

PAINTING A BOTTLE

1 Removing grease
To remove grease and fingermarks, wipe the bottle and stopper with a clean, soft cloth dipped in turpentine.

Glowing Color
A decorative painted design transforms a simple stoppered perfume bottle into a gem.

2 Painting the bottle
Apply glass paint with a fine brush, covering the bottle as evenly as possible. Rinse the brush periodically in turpentine. Coat the stopper in a contrasting color. Let dry.

3 Adding outline designs
Decorate the painted surfaces with simple designs drawn in outline relief paste, applied directly from the tube.

Jeweled Treasures

A spectrum of sparkling, clear colors gives glowing life to a collection of bottles of all shapes and characters. The motifs are simple, for often the simplest ideas – like small gold dots on plain midnight blue – are the most effective, and they need no more skill than a steady hand and a confident touch.

DRIFTWOOD COLLAGE

MATERIALS
- Paper
- Graph paper
- Dry driftwood
- Thin softwood
- Acrylic, gouache, or latex paint
- Water
- PVA glue
- PVA varnish
- Screw eye with ring

I**F YOU HAVE EVER** wandered along a deserted beach thinking deep thoughts, you are likely to have returned home with your pockets heavy with interesting pebbles, sand-blasted shards of glass, and sea–worn strips of painted timber, for which there is no obvious purpose other than to collect dust on a shelf. At last, here is the home for your flotsam; with a touch of paint, a dab of glue, and a cautious wielding of the craft knife, you can create a small masterpiece. The finished collage is charming and unpretentious, and will serve to remind you of many happy hours spent beachcombing, and the particularly slicing northeast wind that brought tears to your eyes on that sunny spring day.

CUTTING THE SHAPES

1 Drawing shapes
Sketch a simple design of a boat and lighthouse. Then draw the shapes on graph paper, aligning the longest side of each shape with the arrow, which represents the wood grain.

2 Cutting shapes from wood
Select a piece of dry driftwood for the background. Mark out the shapes of the design on to pieces of thin softwood (an old fruit crate is ideal). It is easier to cut following the grain; if you cut across the grain, the wood is likely to split. Cut out each piece using a craft knife.

PAINTING

1 Painting background
Paint the driftwood background with a thin wash of turquoise paint. You can use acrylic, gouache, or latex paint, diluted with plenty of water. Apply further coats if desired. Leave to dry.

2 Painting design elements
Paint the separate elements of the design. Here the boat is painted blue, the sails brown, and the lighthouse with black and white stripes. You could also add a stripe of fluorescent paint to the lighthouse if desired. Leave to dry.

ASSEMBLING AND VARNISHING

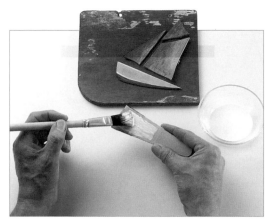

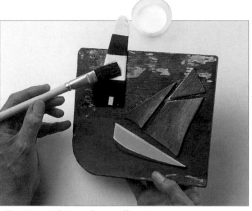

1 Gluing the pieces
Spread PVA glue on the back of each painted piece and place on the driftwood background. Press firmly to secure. Wipe off any excess glue with a cloth. To keep the softwood from warping, place a heavy weight on top of the collage and let dry.

2 Varnishing the collage
Varnish the finished collage with a coat of PVA varnish to seal. Allow to dry. Finally, fix a screw eye with ring attached in the upper center back of the collage to hang it on a wall.

Boat Show
This little collage is perfect for a nautical bathroom – a fleet in different colors bobbing close together looks even better. The best part of it all is that it gives you an unimpeachable excuse to wander the beach, collect flotsam, and sketch boats. Nothing beats personal observation and, while your seafaring friends may scoff, a few scrappy notes will enable you to come up with a slightly more convincing cut of jib and swing of boom. Otherwise, for inspiration as to shape and styles of boats, take a look at magazines aimed at sailing types.

MOSAIC BATHROOM CABINET

WITH A FRISKY FISH motif in lieu of your familiar early morning face, the humble bathroom cabinet can become cheerfully artistic. This mosaic has all the intense color and sparkle of glass, and a lively image, enhanced by the use of different shades of each color. It is small and self-contained and should not daunt the beginner, but be sure to wear goggles and beware of sharp edges as you work. A mosaic center panel is an idea that will apply happily in the kitchen – an herb and spice cabinet with a leafy design would be pretty.

Mosaic scissors

PREPARING THE CABINET

1 Painting the cabinet
Remove the mirror and mount from the cabinet. Paint the cabinet with two coats of blue latex paint. When dry, varnish the surface and let dry.

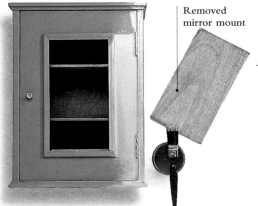
Removed mirror mount

2 Designing the mosaic
Sketch a simple design for the mosaic. Copy it onto the mirror mount using a black marker. Here, the design is of two fish surrounded by a checked border.

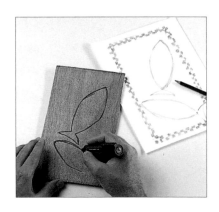

APPLYING THE MOSAIC

1 Cutting glass pieces
Choose the colors of vitreous glass you want to use. Then, using mosaic scissors, cut the glass into small square-shaped pieces. Wear goggles to protect your eyes while cutting the glass.

2 Building up the border
Using a spatula, apply PVA glue onto the marked border on the mount. Lay blue glass in the glue, leaving a gap between each piece to build up the design. Leave a space between the border and the edge of the mount to allow for inserting the mount in the cabinet.

3 Completing the mosaic design

Build up the shapes of the fish using small squares of orange and yellow glass to create a tropical feel. Then fill in the background with pale blue glass.

4 Applying grout

Leave the mosaic to dry for a day. Mix tile grout to mud pie consistency or buy ready-made grout. Using a squeegee, apply grout over the mosaic. Clean off the excess with a damp cloth or sponge. When dry, polish the mosaic with a soft cloth and insert the mount in the cabinet.

Piscean Panel

A pair of Caribbean-bright fish swim in a turquoise sea on the front of this bathroom cabinet. The irregular triangle pieces represent the lively ripples of water, and are contained in a border of blue squares.

APPLIQUÉ LAUNDRY BAG

MATERIALS

- Upholstery fabric
- Strong sewing thread
- Paper
- Remnants of cotton and calico
- Fusible webbing
- Button
- Sewing thread
- 2 pieces of upholstery cord, 62in (1.5m) long

ANYONE WHO HAS SPENT fruitless and frustrating hours trying to find things will know the truth of the Shaker maxim "a place for everything, and everything in its place." This pretty exercise in basic appliqué would make a happy home for half-knitted sweaters and semi-stitched quilts, just as it might draw a decorative veil over your laundry. You will also find that it solves two major problems in one stroke – how to store the excessive acreage of irresistible fabrics that haven't quite been made into garments, and how to use the remains from the garments that have been made.

PREPARING THE BAG

1 Cutting fabric pieces
Cut out two pieces of contrasting upholstery fabric, one piece measuring 32 x 52in (80 x 130cm) and the other measuring 9 x 52in (22 x 130cm). Place the two pieces of fabric with right sides together, then pin and stitch them together along one of the long edges using strong sewing thread.

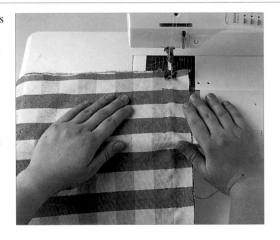

2 Pressing the seam
Carefully and neatly press open the seam with a hot iron, then put the fabric to the side.

STITCHING THE APPLIQUÉ

1 Cutting motifs
Sketch a design for an appliqué motif using simple shapes. Cut out the larger elements from cotton and calico. Before cutting out the smaller elements, back the fabric with fusible webbing (see page 38).

2 Stitching the motifs
Layer the elements of the appliqué motif together, ironing and stitching them to secure. Sew a button in the center of the petals. Vary the stitches and the color of thread for interest.

3 Positioning the appliqué
Turn under the calico edges and press. Position the calico in the center of the large piece of upholstery fabric (see Step 1 above). Stitch in place with blanket stitch using blue sewing thread.

MAKING THE BAG

1 Stitching seams
Turn the fabric right side in and stitch the back seam. Then stitch across the bottom edge so that the back seam is in the center of the bag.

2 Making the opening
Turn down the top edge of the bag 6in (15cm) and mark the position of the buttonholes for the drawstring cord, two buttonholes on each side of the bag. Open the top edge out, stitch the four buttonholes, then turn the edge down again. Stitch two rows 2in (5cm) apart around the top edge.

3 Threading the cord
Thread cord through one opening and out of the other on one side of the bag. Repeat with the other cord on the other side.

Washday Blues

Blue and cream fabric in small and large checks makes a neat receptacle for laundry en route to the laundromat. This Shakerish bag with its sweetly naive motif could be varied by changing fabric and appliqué for different uses – from tiny lavender bags, shoe bags, or decorative sacks to store spare quilts and comforters.

FLOTSAM FRAME

PAINTED DRIFTWOOD HAS a peculiarly appealing quality: flat colors are broken by the action of the water and assume a flaked, speckled fascination; and the grain of the wood is opened to reveal a ridged and furrowed texture that would otherwise require considerable work and effort with a wire brush. There is also something very romantic about pieces of wood that may have floated to your feet from the Indian Ocean or the South China Sea. Be that as it may, painted, weathered rectangles of wood need very little work to transform them into sympathetic frames for the beachcomber's hoard of different subjects.

MATERIALS
Driftwood • Picture
Glue • Cardboard
Acrylic, gouache, or latex paint
Staples • Screw eye with ring

Ocean Blues
A tiny liner on a needlepoint sea is framed in ocean-worn wood, freckled with sapphire and cerulean (right). The narrow edging of terra-cotta around the inside of the frame is a small but significant detail.

MAKING FRAME INSET

1 Collecting driftwood
Collect driftwood from a beach, choosing pieces that are large enough to have a rectangle or square cut out of the center. Leave the driftwood in a warm place to dry.

2 Marking the inset
Glue the picture you want to frame to a piece of cardboard. Measure the area of the picture. Cut a piece of cardboard slightly smaller all around than the picture area and center it on the driftwood. Draw around the cardboard to mark the area to cut out. If the driftwood has paint on it, go over the penciled line with a craft knife; this will prevent flakes of paint from flying around when sawing through the wood.

MAKING THE FRAME

1 Drilling corner holes
Drill a hole in the driftwood in each corner of the marked area. This will allow you to insert the coping saw into the driftwood to saw out the rest of the picture area.

2 Sawing
Insert a coping saw blade through one of the drilled holes in the driftwood. Fix the blade in the coping saw and cut out the picture area by sawing from corner to corner. Do not worry if the sawn edges are uneven.

4 Painting inner edges
Paint the inner smoothed edges of the frame with a coat of terra-cotta paint to contrast with the rest of the frame and the picture. You can use acrylic, gouache, or latex paint. Allow to dry. If you prefer, you could paint the inner edges in a matching color.

3 Sanding rough edges
Trim the inner edges with a utility knife. Then rub a sanding block over the inner edges of the frame to smooth them down.

FRAMING THE PICTURE

1 Aligning the picture
Hold the frame over the picture to check that the frame fits and that the picture is centered. When you are satisfied with the position, hold the picture in place and carefully turn over both frame and picture.

2 Attaching the backing
Staple the cardboard to the back of the frame. Hammer the staples flat if you prefer. Find the upper center of the frame and attach a screw eye with a ring to hang the picture.

DESIGN OPTIONS

This collection of weather-worn little frames is used to launch a flotilla of tapestry boats and flaunt some of the designerish flotsam thrown up by the sea. The driftwood is used just as it comes, or artfully spiked with touches of contrasting color. Needlepoint boats of these diminutive proportions and simple shapes are relatively easy and quick to stitch, or you could frame favorite seaside postcards, prints of rainbow-bright fish, or a real and beautiful shell found at the shoreline.

Weathered Wood

A chunky tug within a square frame of unadorned wood, sanded very slightly around the edges, and picked out in blue within.

Plying the Oceans

A chunk of seaworn plywood, stained brown and rimmed with terra-cotta, makes a dramatic setting for a boat becalmed.

Inky Indigo Seas

A blue so dark as to appear black, with flakes of white and azure, makes an appropriate frame for a ship on a slate blue sea.

Salt and Cinnabar

This plain weatherbeaten pine has been daubed with spontaneous splashes of Shaker blue and cinnabar red.

Boat in a Blizzard

Peeling white paint following the grain of a tideline plank of wood effortlessly evokes an Arctic expedition.

PAINTED TILES

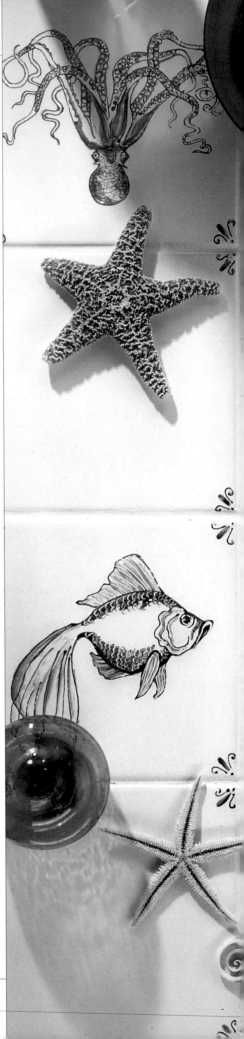

Ceramic paints are a great new discovery. They are simple to use, endlessly adaptable, and they are available in a good range of colors that can be mixed together to create the entire spectrum. With these durable paints you can personalize kitchen and bathroom tiles, as well as decorate plates, bowls, vases, cups, and soap dishes in your own individual style. Because the paint is baked on, it becomes part of the surface of the tile, and will withstand serious scrubbing. You can dilute the paints to make them easier to handle; however, too much water can alter the color.

MATERIALS

Design for tile • Tracing paper
China marker • Ceramic tile
Masking tape • Ceramic paint

TRACING THE DESIGN

1 Choosing a motif
Find a design motif you like and enlarge it if necessary to fit the size of tile you want to decorate. Trace the outline of the motif onto tracing paper using a ballpoint pen or sharp pencil. Here the design is of an octopus.

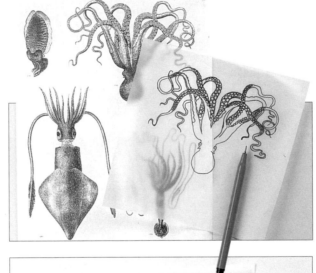

2 Marking the tracing
Turn the tracing paper over and rub a china marker over the traced lines on the reverse side to cover them completely.

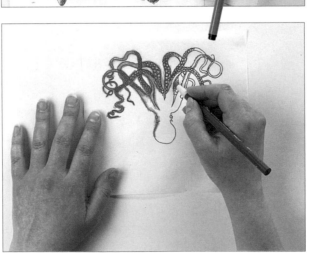

DECORATING THE TILES

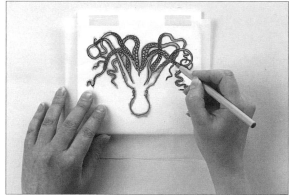

1 Transfer the design
Position the tracing, right side up, over a tile and secure with masking tape. Then draw over the lines of the motif again with a ballpoint pen or sharp pencil to transfer the motif to the tile. Lift up the paper as you go to check for missed lines.

2 Motif check
When you are sure that no parts of the design have been overlooked, remove the tracing paper and the image of the motif will be visible on the tile.

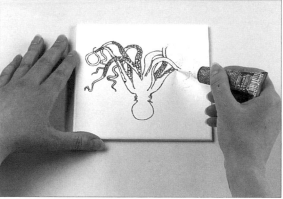

3 Painting the motif
Using a tube of ceramic paint, paint over the outline of the motif on the tile. Squeeze the tube gently for an even flow of paint and to avoid blobs. If you make a mistake, wipe off the paint with a soft cloth. Repeat to decorate as many tiles as you desire. Bake the tiles in an oven to set the paint, following the manufacturer's instructions.

Fishy Business

Delft blue octopuses, crabs, and sundry exotic-looking fish make an appropriately watery theme for bathroom tiles (left). Little curlicues in the corners of each tile build up to form a charming and whimsical nosegay pattern.

DECORATIVE EXTRAS

ONCE YOU HAVE discovered the joys of ceramic paint, nothing will be safe. Any paint effect that you can achieve with ordinary paints or glazes can be tackled with ceramic paint, but the results are interestingly unpredictable. If you are planning to embellish a large area with tiles, it would be a good idea to experiment with a load of cheap chipped rejects before you commit yourself to acres of mistakes. The paint dries to a satisfyingly hard and glossy finish; it would not last on a floor, and might expire under repeated scrubbing with an abrasive cleaner, but in a bathroom where an occasional wipe is all that is needed for sink surrounds and backsplashes, it will survive with aplomb. Another point to bear in mind when painting tiles is that it is a good idea to follow the manufacturer's instructions exactly, since errors such as the wrong oven temperature are likely to change the color to its detriment. You can mix the colors of ceramic paints, but diluting them with water does them no favors. The colors straight from the bottle are vibrant enough to look great on their own, just painted evenly as they come. Alternatively, painting a patchwork of different colors can also look wonderful in a sunny Mediterranean sort of way.

Painting with a Tube

It is quite easy to paint tiles simply by squeezing ceramic paint from a tube, though you will probably need to practice first to get an even pressure on the tube. By applying paint in this way, you can produce raised squiggles, dots, and fine lines, which are perfect for outlining. The moon design was transferred from a book. After completing the raised outlines, painting in the solid colors was comparatively easy. If you do make a mistake, simply wipe off the paint with a damp cloth and start again. The stripy design was copied from some Moroccan pots, then transferred onto the tile using a pencil and ruler.

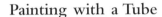

- *When painting a tile, start from the top to avoid smudging the paint. If outlining a design, work slowly to achieve an even line. When dry, use an artist's brush to apply paint in between outlines for a neat effect.*

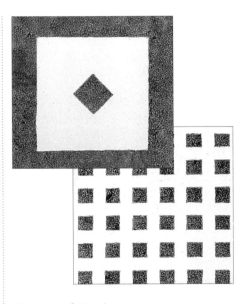

Sponged Variants

Sponging is an extremely simple and effective method of applying paint onto tiles, and works especially well when used in combination with stencils. The two tiles above were both sponged using very basic stenciling techniques. The gray diamond at the top was delineated with masking tape. The bottom tile, with its grid of squares, was created by laying strips of masking tape up and down and across the tile. After sponging on the ceramic paint, the strips of masking tape were carefully peeled off to reveal the stencil pattern beneath.

- *To sponge a tile, dip a sponge in a saucer of ceramic paint, and dab it on a paper towel to remove excess paint. Then dab the sponge over the tile to cover the entire surface, adding more paint when necessary.*

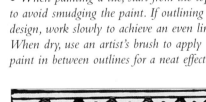
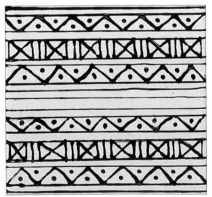

Egyptian Fish

A smiling fish of indeterminate species in a sea of blue would be appropriate for either a bathroom or a kitchen. This one was copied from an ancient piece of sculpture, drawn in freehand straight onto the tile and outlined in blue. Then the scales were painted, the blue background was sponged, and bronze flecks were added to evoke flakes of sunlight in Mediterranean waters.

• *When using more than one color, allow the first color to dry before applying the next so the colors do not mix or run. Use an artist's brush to paint the fish, being careful not to smudge the colors. Let dry, then paint the background with a sponge dipped in paint to create a soft, dappled effect.*

Dragged Tile

If utterly plain, solidly painted tiles seem too boring to bother with, you could give them a subtle texture by dragging paint over the tiles with a wide household paintbrush, which results in discreet stripes. You then have the choice of laying them all in the same direction, or making a patchwork with the stripes at right angles to each other.

• *To create a dragged effect on a tile, apply the ceramic paint thickly on the tile and brush slowly in one direction only, dragging the paint along. Keep an even pressure on the paintbrush to ensure even stripes.*

Spotted Fruit and Hearts

Filched from a William Morris design, this pomegranate was drawn with cobalt blue ceramic paint, then filled in with a concentric dot pattern. The simple heart motif was drawn with a tube liner, then shadowed with dots. One of the secrets of successful painting is the importance of texture. Flat, matte color has its role, but it is more interesting to distress, age, or fill in, with your paint finishes.

• *To add interest to a simple painted motif, paint dots within the shape to create patterns, or outline the motif with dots to create the effect of shadow and three dimensions.*

Stenciled Tiles

A repeating stencil can provide a simple and effective method of painting a tile. Choose a star motif, a flower motif as here, or a more geometric design. Don't worry if your stencil is not entirely symmetrical. Perfect accuracy is not the point; you can buy perfect tiles if you want them, but yours will bear their handmade signature with pride. If desired, you can change the base color of your tile before stenciling.

• *To make a simple repeating stencil suitable for a tile, cut a piece of squared paper the same size as the tile. Fold this diagonally twice and cut shapes out of the paper along the foldlines. When you open out the paper, you will have a symmetrical template. Trace this design onto acetate and cut it out neatly with a craft knife to make the stencil.*

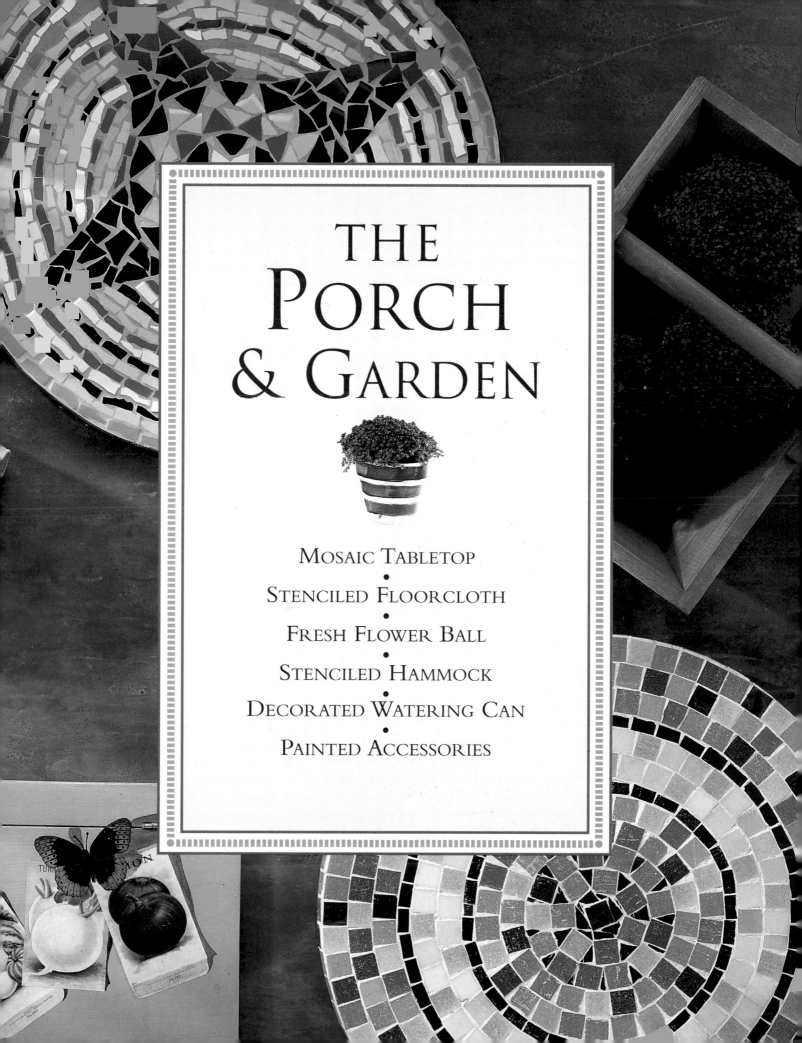

THE PORCH & GARDEN

MOSAIC TABLETOP
•
STENCILED FLOORCLOTH
•
FRESH FLOWER BALL
•
STENCILED HAMMOCK
•
DECORATED WATERING CAN
•
PAINTED ACCESSORIES

MOSAIC TABLETOP

Mosaic scissors

THIS SPARKLING TABLETOP is a real *pièce de résistance*. Tackle it fearlessly and with gusto; mosaic is not difficult, it just needs patience, a bold design for success, and a pair of goggles for safety. For the thrifty-minded, it is a wonderfully economic way to use up the odd, chipped, and broken tiles that stores are eager to sell off. Make sure that the tiles are all the same thickness and finish, though, or the surface of the table will be uneven. Here the central motif is made up of larger, distinct triangles to give emphasis and crisp definition. A small object like this tabletop can look somewhat chaotic unless the color range is limited. The tiles here are confined to complementary nautical blues and white. The fillet of lead around the tabletop makes a neat, easy, and professional-looking finish.

Mariner's Mosaic

A seafarer's compass inspired this table, a strong motif in a variety of cool blues that would be the perfect perch for a croissant and coffee in the garden, or a plant or two in the porch.

PREPARING THE MOSAIC

1 Drawing design outline
Using a marker, draw a simple design for the mosaic on top of the circular tabletop. This compass design is composed of triangles and concentric circles.

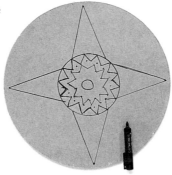

2 Cutting tiles
Using mosaic scissors, cut ceramic tiles into small pieces for the central design, and rectangles for the border circles. Wear goggles to protect your eyes while cutting the tiles.

APPLYING THE MOSAIC AND EDGING

1 Building up the pattern
Use a spatula to apply PVA glue onto the marked central design on the tabletop. Place pieces of tile onto the glue, leaving a slight gap between pieces, to build up the central pattern (see inset). Then build up the surrounding area with a pattern of circles. Use the mosaic scissors to "nibble" the tiles into smaller shapes as desired.

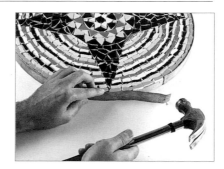

2 Edging with lead
Wrap a strip of lead around the tabletop and cut it to fit exactly, using a pair of scissors. Secure the lead to the tabletop by hammering in nails at 4 in (10 cm) intervals around the circumference, and then a couple at each end.

3 Grouting the mosaic
Leave the mosaic to dry for a day. Apply gray tile grout (mixed to mud pie consistency) over the mosaic with a squeegee. Clean off the excess with a damp cloth or sponge. When dry, polish with a soft cloth and attach the tabletop to the base.

DESIGN OPTIONS

Concentric Circles
Circles of speckled color in sea greens and stone combine in a very simple but effective design.

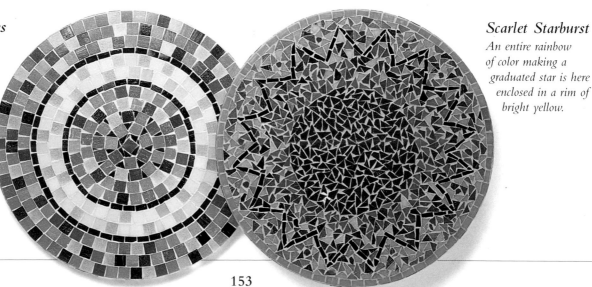

Scarlet Starburst
An entire rainbow of color making a graduated star is here enclosed in a rim of bright yellow.

STENCILED FLOORCLOTH

PAINTED CANVAS FLOORCLOTHS, often nautical in inspiration, brightened the outlook in the homes of countless early American settlers. They are not at all difficult to make, are surprisingly durable, and bring a welcome touch of comfort and color to the austere, cool, and practical flooring of the porch. One secret is to use as many layers of varnish as you have patience for; not only do these protect the cloth but they also give it a necessary stiffness. Ironing the canvas to start with is probably the most onerous part of the process; the rest is pure pleasure. If you want to make a larger floorcloth, you can tape it to a tabletop or a washable floor while you paint.

MATERIALS

Canvas, approximately 4 x 2ft (1.2m x 60cm) • Acrylic primer
Latex paint: turquoise, green, white, blue • Masking tape
Household sponge • Small block of wood • Water • Latex glue
Stencils (*see page 219*) • Acrylic floor varnish

PREPARING THE CANVAS

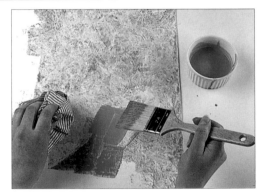

1 Stretching the canvas
Cut out a piece of canvas of the required size. Iron out any noticeable creases. Trim away the selvages. Stretch the canvas over a wooden frame and staple the edges to the frame so that the canvas is taut.

2 Gluing the edges
Paint four coats of diluted acrylic primer over the canvas front. When dry, remove it from the frame and place it painted side down. Stick the edges down with latex glue. Paint two coats of acrylic primer over the back.

3 Creating a textured surface
Brush diluted turquoise latex paint quickly over the surface of the floorcloth. Dab the wet paint with a crumpled soft cloth to create a textured effect.

Fearlessly Faux
This elegant floorcloth looks like marble but is just canvas and paint. It looks three-dimensional but is as flat as paper.

MAKING THE BORDER

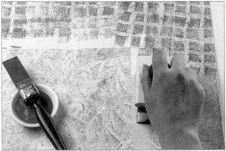

1 Making a printing block
Make a simple printing block from a household sponge by cutting pieces out of the sponge with a utility knife. This printing block is in the shape of a grid. Glue the back of the sponge to a block of wood to create a firm printing block.

2 Printing the floorcloth
Mask off an area around the edge of the floorcloth to be the border. Paint the cut side of the printing sponge with green paint, then press the sponge onto the border area to make a print. Repeat to print over the entire border. Add more paint to the sponge as you need it. Allow to dry.

3 Stenciling the border
Position the stencil (see page 219) over the top of the printed border area, then paint over the stencil in green paint. For an even finish, use a paint roller to apply the paint, rolling off excess paint onto a paper towel before painting over the stencil to avoid drips. Let it dry.

MAKING THE CENTRAL PANEL

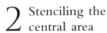

1 Marbling
Remove the masking tape and apply new strips of tape on the inside of the border so that you can paint the central panel of the floorcloth. Paint thin, jagged diagonal lines of white latex paint over the central panel to give the effect of marbling. Let it dry.

2 Stenciling the central area
Stencil the central area using diagonal stencils (see page 218). Use a paint roller and apply first green, then blue, latex paint to create the pattern of tumbling blocks. Allow to dry.

3 Edging the floorcloth
Mask off the outer and inner border edges with masking tape. Apply turquoise latex paint in between the taped lines and at the edge of the floorcloth to create thin straight stripes. These stripes emphasize the two areas of decoration on the floorcloth and sharpen the overall design.

4 Finishing the floorcloth
When dry, apply three coats of acrylic floor varnish. Allow the floorcloth to dry for four days before using it.

DESIGN OPTIONS

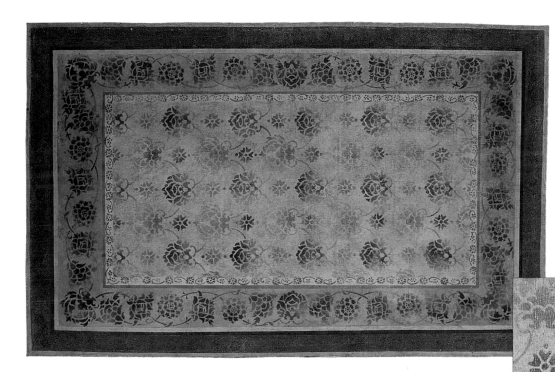

Flowers at your Feet

Stylized floral motifs regularly spaced and stenciled in misty mutable colors adorn a floorcloth (left and below) that would not have looked out of place in Jane Austen's front parlor. The colors have a common denominator of burnt umber, which smooths out any hint of brashness, and the careful design is enhanced by bands and stripes so that it has all the richness and discipline of a Persian rug.

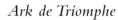

Ark de Triomphe

An elegant menagerie of mythical beasts stalks this trio of floorcloths (below) in refined and subtle shades. The stenciled designs are sophisticated and beautifully drawn but copyable. The harmony of the colors, both singly and en masse, is augmented by the broken and distressed finish, and a discreet homogenizing layer of burnt umber to tone down the raw paint.

FRESH FLOWER BALL

MATERIALS
- Ball-shaped florist's foam
- Water
- Dowels
- Fresh flowers
- Thick cord
- Adhesive tape

THE BEAUTY OF FRESH flowers is fleeting, but all the more seductive for that. This ball of young, unfurled rosebuds and cornfield flowers expresses all the promise of the first days of summer, and is reminiscent of old-fashioned flower balls, whose sunny yellow pompoms were composed entirely of cowslips, with which country girls traditionally used to guess the identity of their husbands-to-be. What fresh flowers have is scent and texture – dried or silk flowers last forever, but you never want to bury your nose in them, or stroke their velvety petals. These pretty posies are an extravagant gesture that is just right for a summer wedding or to say thank you.

Innocent Pastels

The essence of innocence, fresh cornflowers and rosebuds are the main components of this fragrant floral decoration.

MAKING THE FLOWER BALL

1 Inserting dowel
Soak the flower foam in water for an hour. Insert a piece of dowel through the center of the foam, so that it protrudes out of the opposite side. Rest the two ends of the dowel on supports so that the florist's foam is suspended.

2 Cutting the flowers
Using sharp scissors, trim the fresh flowers so that their stalks are 2 in (5 cm) long. Cut the stalks at an angle to allow them to take up water more easily. Reserve a piece of stalk 2 in (5 cm) long for use in Step 5.

3 Arranging the flowers
Begin to arrange the flowers and foliage in the florist's foam. Starting with stems of background foliage, push the stalks a short way into the foam all over the ball, retaining the spherical shape.

4 Filling in gaps

Continue to insert flowers and foliage in the flower ball until no foam is visible. Arrange the different flowers evenly over the ball so that the end result is a pleasing combination of colors and shapes. This flower ball follows a color theme of yellows, pinks, and greens.

5 Attaching the cord

Tie one end of a length of thick cord securely around the piece of stalk reserved in Step 2. The cord will be used to hang the flower ball.

6 Inserting the cord

Attach the other end of the cord to one end of the dowel using adhesive tape. Then carefully pull the dowel out of the flower ball, so that the cord is pulled through the ball with it. The stalk will prevent the end of the cord from going through the flower ball.

7 Adjusting the flower ball

Remove the dowel from the cord and hang the flower ball from a doorway, archway, or ceiling. Then check the flower ball to ensure that the overall balance is satisfactory, rearranging flowers if necessary to achieve a pleasing result.

DESIGN OPTIONS

Festive Tree

Daisies, violets, clematis whorls, and poppy heads, set on top of a trunk of cinnamon sticks, make a neat tribute to spring in a painted pot, as a floral focal point for table or windowsill. Rough twigs and meadow flowers in a terra-cotta pot would make a rustic version.

Great Ball of Flowers

A dramatic sunburst of red dianthus and gloriosa lilies, with yellow rosebuds and frilled carnations, makes a sophisticated centerpiece for a grand dinner, or to hang from a chandelier at Christmas.

STENCILED HAMMOCK

MATERIALS

- Heavy duty canvas, approximately 2¼ yd x 44 in (2 x 1.1 m)
- Water
- Strong cotton
- 2 dowels 62 in (1.5 m) long and 1 in (2.5 cm) thick
- Stencils *(see page 220)*
- Fabric paint: blue, green, brown, pink
- Masking tape
- Strong rope

Few experiences are more relaxing than lazing in a hammock under trees, shaded from the noonday sun. This project is emphatically a one-person hammock intended for the precarious lengthwise balance, but you might want to experiment with more generous widths, gathering the ends with strong brass eyelets and rope to provide a more than solitary snooze.

On this design the shell, dolphin, and seaweed motifs combine gracefully and have a breezy outdoor feel. Stenciling on fabric is easy to do with the magical new fabric paints that are available. It only takes a quick pass with an iron to fix the color, and the technique shown here adapts itself uncomplainingly to many fabrics and functions. This canvas design, for example, could, without major changes, become an ornate bathroom blind. The rope and shells could just as easily make a nautical border for a plain cotton tablecloth.

PREPARING THE FABRIC

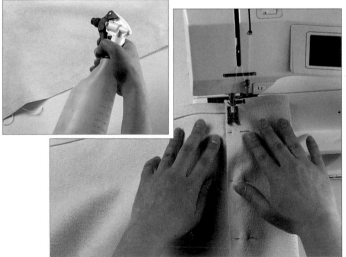

1 Preshrinking the canvas
Trim away the selvages from the canvas. Spray the canvas with water to preshrink it. If you do not do this, the canvas may buckle while you are painting it. Leave to dry.

2 Hemming the hammock
Turn under the long sides of the canvas by 1 in (2.5 cm) and machine stitch two rows with strong cotton. Turn under 3½ in (9 cm) at each short end of the canvas and again stitch two rows with strong cotton. Be sure that the dowel fits into the turnover at each short end.

STENCILING THE BORDER

1 Applying the color
Tape the border stencil (see page 220) to the canvas edge. Stipple blue and green fabric paint through the stencil, overlapping colors.

2 Mitering a corner
Stick a strip of masking tape at an angle of 45 degrees across the corner of the stencil and paint up to this edge. Then replace the stencil along the adjoining edge of canvas, and lay another strip of tape at the same angle over the top before continuing.

COMPLETING THE HAMMOCK

1 Stenciling shells
When the border is dry, stencil the shell designs (see page 220) inside the border. Use a selection of brown, greenish-brown, and pink fabric paints. Carefully remove the stencil and allow the paints to dry.

2 Completing the design
Paint over the shells with dilute brown fabric paint to soften the white areas. Stencil the dolphins and seaweed. When dry, iron the back of the canvas with a hot iron to fix the paint. Insert dowels through the turnovers, drill a hole in each dowel end, and thread with strong rope to hang the hammock from.

Swinging Shells

At its most basic, a hammock is just a rectangle of strong cloth strung between two trees. Anyone who has ever persevered with the art of hammock-lounging will have become a committed devotee. Here, shells and dolphins suggest exotic waters — all you need to add is palm trees and a coral beach. Dream on…

DECORATED WATERING CAN

MATERIALS
- Tracing paper
- Galvanized steel watering can
- White primer
- Yellow gloss paint
- Masking tape
- Acrylic paint: blue, dark blue

AN EXTENSION OF THE FINE art of toleware, this watering can decorated in vibrant blue and yellow knocks its plain galvanized beginnings into the shade. Humble metal objects can look as rich and costly as you have a mind and the patience to make them. They can blend easily into a traditional country-house look with an overlay of paisley colors, they can be as sharp as city slang in sizzling orange and lime, or they can be as fresh as spring with echoes of bluebells, tulips, and miniature daffodils. All it takes is paint, a brush, and a little confidence.

Summer Colors

Painted with a simple blue pattern on a sunny yellow base, this watering can would make a cheerful addition to a porch.

PREPARING THE WATERING CAN

1 Tracing the pattern

Trace a suitable pattern with which to decorate the watering can. This design came from an old pattern book. Turn the tracing over and go over the outlines with a soft pencil to enable you to transfer the design onto the watering can.

2 Cleaning the surface

Using a soft cloth, clean the outside of the watering can thoroughly to remove any dirt and grease from the metal surface, which would prevent the paint from adhering.

3 Applying primer

Using a household paintbrush, paint an even layer of white primer over the outer surface of the metal watering can, including the spout, handle, and lid. Let dry.

PAINTING THE WATERING CAN

1 Applying gloss paint
Paint a coat of yellow gloss paint over the watering can, then let dry. If any areas of primer are still visible, fill in with paint.

2 Transferring the design
Secure the tracing to the side of the watering can with masking tape. Then pencil over all the outlines of the design to transfer it to the can.

3 Painting the design
Remove the tracing. Using an artist's brush and pale blue acrylic paint, paint the details.

4 Adding more decoration
Paint dots and a line around the base of the watering can and along the handle. Then add more definition to the painted decoration using dark blue acrylic paint.

5 Joining the dots
Paint rings of color around the spout of the watering can to echo the main decoration. Then complete the detailing on the handle by joining the rows of dots with fine dark blue lines. Let dry.

DESIGN OPTIONS

Sprigged Nightlight
Tiny indigo and scarlet flowers painted onto a sky blue candle holder have a nursery rhyme simplicity and charm. Old metal objects can often spring to life with a splash of panache.

Pretty Plant Holder
Bright tulips in a Ming vase make a delightful contrast with the buttercups or lacy maidenhair fern for which this is intended. Presentation is crucial to enjoying life's lovely things – plants mean so much more in the right surroundings.

PAINTED ACCESSORIES

A SUNROOM, AN ENCLOSED porch, or a summer house is a wonderful thing to have. But all of them have an irresistible magnetism for unattractive bits and pieces - pruning shears, gardening gloves, tattered seed packets, unruly balls of string, woolly socks, and rubber boots – which tend to congregate on floor and shelves in a highly visible way. The answer, as so often, is to put all the small untidy things in custom-made containers whose external charms hide the atrocities within. A coordinated color theme in fresh blues and greens – not matching, but related – holds the whole ensemble together, and gives it all the air of a sunny spring day. If you can carry your ideas through to window blinds and plant pots, you should be able to bask in utter harmony.

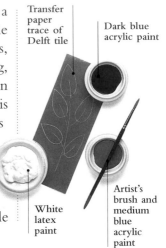

Transfer paper trace of Delft tile

Dark blue acrylic paint

White latex paint

Artist's brush and medium blue acrylic paint

LEAF SPRAY DRAWERS

The perfect hiding place for scruffy seed packets and scarlet plastic pruning knives, this plywood chest of drawers can be decorated very quickly with a repeat pattern of leafy twigs. The design was borrowed from a Delft tile, and painted in the same two shades of blue on a white background.

1 Painting the dots
Paint the outside of the chest white. When dry, remove the drawers and, using an artist's brush, paint blue dots in between the drawers.

2 Adding leafy design
Using the same color blue acrylic paint, paint a simple pattern of leaves and twigs – or trace the design from an enlarged photocopy and then paint over it – along each of the drawer fronts. Outline the leaves and twigs and add leaf veins with darker blue acrylic paint. When dry, coat with matte acrylic varnish to seal.

164

SEA-GREEN TRUG

This is what every gardener needs on pottering expeditions to carry all the tools down to the far end of the garden and bring back a bouquet of graceful rosebuds – or the odd tennis balls that have been revealed by the bare branches of winter.

Blue acrylic paint

Masking tape

Green wood stain

Blue wood stain

Artist's brush

Paintbrush

Painting the trug

Paint the trug with several layers of dilute blue and green wood stain to achieve an ocean blue color, and let dry. Then stick two lengths of masking tape down the sides of the trug separated by a narrow gap, and paint in between with blue acrylic paint.

TROMPE-L'OEIL TOOLBOX

This small blue box has a Shakerish plainness, which has been enlivened by a flurry of photocopied butterflies and old-fashioned seed packets. A shapely terra-cotta plant label is a very basic exercise in *trompe-l'oeil*, along with the shadows that give a hint of three dimensions. The trick is to lay out the elements and sketch them in place, using a strong side light to draw in the shadows.

Paper motifs

Acrylic paint

Decorative seed packets

PVA glue

Varnish

Artist's brush

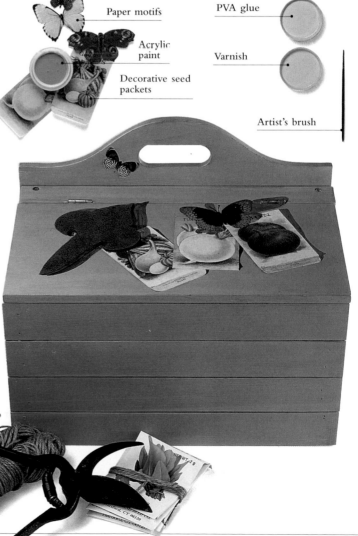

1 Drawing in shadows
Position a collection of three-dimensional objects on the painted box lid. Then direct a light at the lid from one side of the box so that shadows are cast from the objects. Draw around the objects and shadows with a pencil, and then paint them in with acrylic paint.

2 Adding découpage decoration
When the paint is dry, glue decorative paper cutouts and seed packets in position with PVA glue. When dry, varnish the toolbox with matte acrylic varnish to seal.

SPOTTED FLOWERPOT

This terra-cotta plant pot was simply painted with ceramic paint, and sealed in an ordinary domestic oven to a bright, glossy finish. Make sure the pot is dry before painting it, or the paint will bubble and misbehave. You could make a set of pots planted with daisies or miniature roses to parade down the center of a conservatory table.

Dark blue ceramic paint

Terra-cotta plant pot

White ceramic paint

Decorating the pot
Paint the pot with blue ceramic paint and, when dry, paint large white spots around the rim of the pot using a fine artist's brush. Bake the pot in an oven to seal the paint, following the manufacturer's instructions.

TULIP SHELF

Jaunty tulips, beloved by the Pennsylvania Dutch, make a lively and colorful horticultural frieze for a hinged shelf front – just the thing to store bulbs over winter. However, you do not need to be a Dutch master to paint tulips like these. Tulips have the great advantage of being very easy to draw, and shades of different-colored paint for flowers and leaves make them casually convincing.

Dark brown acrylic paint

Artist's brush

Pencil

Green acrylic paint

Red acrylic paint

Blue acrylic paint

Varnish

Sketch of pattern

Yellow acrylic paint

Decorating the shelf
Paint the shelf blue; when dry, paint a row of tulips freehand – or trace the tulips below – using yellow, red, green, and brown paint. Finally, varnish the shelf to seal.

FLEUR-DE-LIS PLANTER

The bold indigo motif on this plywood planter was taken from a book on heraldry. It was painted onto a green wash and highlighted with delicate flashes of silver. An obelisk of clipped box tree would be quite at home in this painted planter, which has a practical zinc base to withstand judicious watering.

Painting the planter

Look for interesting motifs in books on heraldry or other reference material. Sketch or trace the design, adapting it to fit the size of planter. Cover the planter with a diluted green paint and leave to dry. Transfer the design onto the planter using carbon paper and a pencil. Paint in the details using acrylic paint and an artist's brush, adding flashes of silver paint to enliven the design. Seal the planter with matte acrylic varnish to finish.

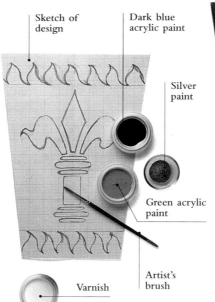

Sketch of design

Dark blue acrylic paint

Silver paint

Green acrylic paint

Varnish

Artist's brush

VERDIGRIS SEAT

If your budget does not run to elaborate wrought-metal seats, you can fake the patina of oxidized copper using a cunning mixture of green paints over a darker base coat. There are many ways to give a much-weathered look to brand-new wooden furniture. Having tackled bronze, you might like to fake old lead or rusted iron.

Dark green latex paint

Pale green latex paint

Mint green latex paint

Gray latex paint

Bronze paint

1 Stippling on green paint
Paint the seat with a coat of dark green latex paint. When dry, stipple on a layer of paler green paint using a stencil brush. Then stipple on a layer of mint green latex paint.

2 Dusting on gray paint
When dry, lightly dab gray paint over the seat using a decorator's stippling brush to apply the paint very faintly. Finally, add a few smudges of bronze paint to give the look of old metal.

BLIND FAITH

Fabric painting is trickier than painting on wood because you cannot paint out your mistakes; wood can cope with any number of layers of corrective color without betraying your secret splodges. But masking tape ensures a crisp, straight stripe, and you can achieve a wonderful blend of subtle color with translucent fabric paint. Here, a combination of geometry and nature makes a seductive bouquet to hang at your windows.

Painting stripes and squares
Lay the blind canvas down flat and stick lengths of masking tape lengthwise over the fabric, leaving even spaces between strips. Paint between the tape strips with fabric paint to achieve neat, straight stripes. For a grid pattern, add widthwise lengths of masking tape across the lengthwise stripes and paint between these. Iron the canvas on the reverse side to set the paint.

MONOGRAMMED SHELF

You can never have too many shelves – this one has a useful row of pegs from which to hang rakes, brooms, and other garden paraphernalia from loops of leather. The swashed initials were copied from an antique hope chest, and the delicate edging came from a picture frame. Painting tiny repeat motifs like this requires a fluent line and a relaxed hand. You may find it an easier operation to paint the shelf before it is assembled.

Painting the shelf
Paint the shelf with pale blue acrylic paint. When dry, sketch the initial letters in pencil in the center of the shelf, then paint them dark blue; it is a good idea to practice on cardboard first. Paint the edging around the top of the shelf in the same color. Let dry.

Masking tape

Pale green acrylic paint

Pale blue acrylic paint

Paintbrush

Artist's brush

Pale blue acrylic paint

Dark blue acrylic paint

Artist's brush

Paintbrush

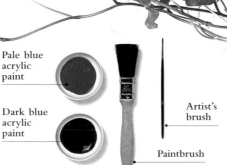

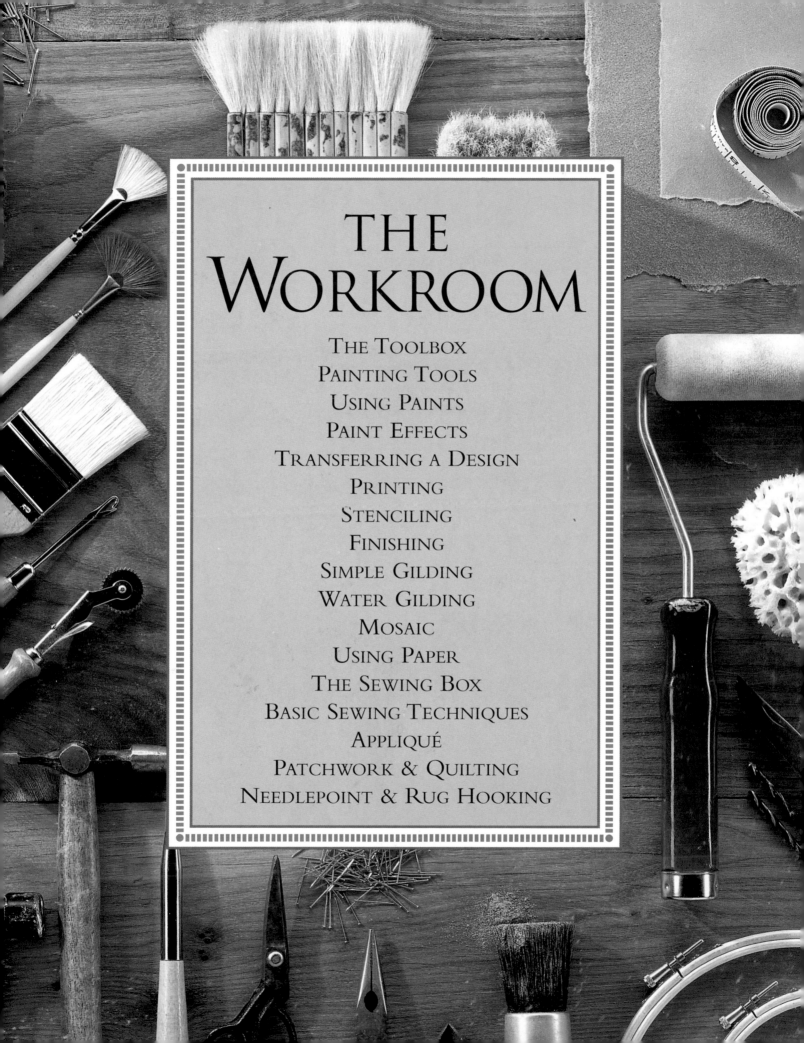

THE
WORKROOM

THE TOOLBOX
PAINTING TOOLS
USING PAINTS
PAINT EFFECTS
TRANSFERRING A DESIGN
PRINTING
STENCILING
FINISHING
SIMPLE GILDING
WATER GILDING
MOSAIC
USING PAPER
THE SEWING BOX
BASIC SEWING TECHNIQUES
APPLIQUÉ
PATCHWORK & QUILTING
NEEDLEPOINT & RUG HOOKING

THE TOOLBOX

ALTHOUGH EACH individual craft will require its own list of specialty tools and equipment, it is advisable to have a basic toolbox stocked with general tools. Whether you simply want to hammer in a nail, or cut out paper motifs, you need the tools to do it with, and a place where you can store them.

The tools shown here are not expensive to buy and are readily available at do-it-yourself stores. Always buy the best you can afford: Poor-quality tools will give your work a shoddy finish. Although it seems obvious, do ensure that you use the right tool for the job. In this way, the straightforward tasks of cutting, gluing, and hammering become easier, quicker, safer, and more effective. Finally, once you have invested in your toolbox essentials, look after them, and they will last for years.

MEASURING AND MARKING

In all types of crafts, accurate measuring and marking are essential to achieve a neat finish.

A hard pencil makes fine lines on wood and paper, but these can be hard to erase.

An eraser will remove pencil marks, and some inks.

A soft pencil is good for broad marks and for shading.

Felt-tip pens, some of which leave permanent marks, work well on shiny surfaces such as tiles.

A steel ruler is useful for cutting straight edges with a craft knife, as well as for measuring and marking.

CUTTING

Keep cutting tools sharp, and use them with care. Never cut toward your fingers.

A scalpel has a very sharp blade, ideal for cutting paper or acetate.

A craft knife's tubular handle allows it to be turned to cut out intricate shapes.

Small scissors should be used on paper and fabric for fine cutting.

Thick cardboard and tough material should be cut with a heavy duty utility knife.

A hacksaw will cut through wood and metal. Use the right blade for each material.

Paper shears work best for cutting long straight or curving edges.

STICKING DOWN

When choosing adhesives and tapes, consider the surfaces to be adhered and whether it is to be temporary or permanent.

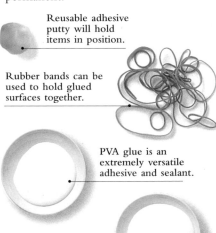

Reusable adhesive putty will hold items in position.

Rubber bands can be used to hold glued surfaces together.

PVA glue is an extremely versatile adhesive and sealant.

Wood glue is the best adhesive for wood.

Clear tape works well on paper and cardboard, but can damage paintwork.

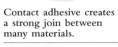

Contact adhesive creates a strong join between many materials.

Low-tack masking tape will not damage delicate or painted surfaces.

THE TOOLBOX

ATTACHING AND HOLDING

Many methods of joining materials together, such as molding pins, work best in combination with an appropriate glue.

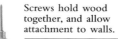

Screws hold wood together, and allow attachment to walls.

A staple will hold cardboard and thin wood, and will attach fabric to wood.

An awl will start a hole for nails or screws.

Match the screwdriver tip and size to the screw, or you will wreck the screw.

Molding pins are used for light items and to hold glued wood in place.

Steel tacks have large heads and will hold fabric in place without pulling through.

A tack hammer has a small head and is for hammering pins, tacks, and small nails.

ELECTRIC DRILL

An electric drill is primarily used for drilling holes in wood and metal, and the right size and type of drill bit should always be used. There are also other attachments available, including grinding, sanding, and polishing tools, that greatly speed up an arduous task.

SMOOTHING SURFACES

The secret of achieving a good painted, waxed, or varnished finish lies in the preparation of the surface. Time put into sanding is time well spent, and these are the tools to help you.

Coarse steel wool removes loose material from rough surfaces.

Fine steel wool produces a smoother surface and can be used to apply wax.

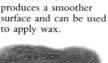

Sandpaper comes in a range of grades. Used for smoothing wood, it can also be used to distress paintwork.

Also available in a range of grades, wet-and-dry paper is good for smoothing paint. It gives a glass-smooth surface.

CLEANING

Before any decorating, ensure that the surface is clean and dry, and always have a cloth on hand in case of mistakes.

Use a household cloth or rag to clean surfaces and wipe spills.

A lint-free cloth will remove dust to prepare the surface for finishing.

PAINTING TOOLS

THERE ARE MANY different tools available for painting furniture and accessories; a selection of these tools are featured here. In addition to general household paintbrushes and paint rollers, you can use artist's brushes, stippling brushes, sponges, combs, and stencil brushes, all of which are designed to produce specific decorative effects.

Always keep a few different-sized household paintbrushes for general painting. A paint roller is also useful for painting small flat surfaces. Artist's brushes are essential for painting fine lines or decorative patterns; select the bristle sizes most useful to you. If you want to create textured paint finishes, you can choose from a wide range of different tools and brushes. Use stencil brushes for dabbing or rubbing paint through a cut stencil. To soften brushmarks and create a mottled effect, use a soft-bristled stippling brush. Apply paint with a natural or synthetic sponge to produce a characteristic textured finish; you can also create a pattern of lines on a surface by pulling a rubber comb through wet glaze.

Build up your stock of painting tools gradually, buying as good a quality as you can. Always clean your brushes after use and hang them up to store, so that their bristles do not lose their shape. If you take care of your paintbrushes, they will last for years.

GENERAL PAINTING

Brushes for painting large flat areas come in a range of sizes. A paint roller is an efficient alternative. More detailed paintwork requires a narrower brush. Cheap brushes are a false economy, as they lose bristles that must be removed from the surface.

A paint roller and tray will enable you to cover large areas, but a brush is still needed for edges and corners.

Use a wide paintbrush to cover large flat areas.

A narrower brush is needed for more intricate surfaces.

DECORATIVE PAINTING

Use artist's brushes for painting decorative patterns on a small scale. They are available with a variety of different-sized bristles. Choose the size that is suitable for the thickness of line you require.

A fine freehand design requires a very fine artist's brush.

For edges and thicker lines, use a medium brush.

A thicker brush can be used to fill in small areas.

CREATING TEXTURED FINISHES

There are several specialized painting tools available for creating textured paint finishes, ranging from brushes and combs to sponges and cloths. Choose the finish you like, and then the tool you need to create it.

Use a stippling brush to soften brushmarks and create a mottled look.

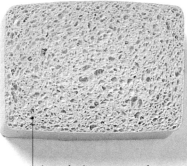

Apply paint with a natural sponge for an irregular texture.

Pull a rubber comb through wet glaze to create a pattern of ridged lines. A range of combs is available.

Dab a scrunched cloth over wet paint to lift it and reveal patches of the base coat.

A synthetic sponge used to dab on paint will create a more even mottled effect.

Stencil brushes, available in a range of sizes, have stiff bristles for dabbing paint through a cut stencil without forcing paint under the edges.

CARING FOR BRUSHES

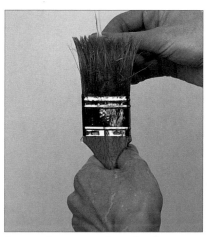

Removing water-based paint
Always clean your paintbrushes after use. To remove water-based paint, hold the brush under running water, working the water through the bristles with your fingers until the water runs clear.

Removing oil-based paint
To remove oil-based paint, swill the brush in a jar of turpentine, working the bristles against the jar sides until the paint comes off and the bristles are clean. Rinse the brush in clean, running water.

Storing brushes
Suspend cleaned brushes on hooks so that the bristles hang down. This helps the brushes keep their shape and prevents the bristles from being damaged.

USING PAINTS

THE TWO BASIC categories of paint are water-based and oil-based. Within these categories are many different paints suitable for different surfaces, finishes, and opacity. To help you choose the type of paint best suited for a particular purpose, paints can be divided into three distinct groups as follows. For general painting of surfaces, whether wood, MDF, metal, or plastic, choose paints from the general painting group, which include latex, oil-based, acrylic, and spray paint. For painting special surfaces, such as ceramic, fabric, and glass, you need paints specially formulated for those surfaces. For creating unusual paint effects on a surface, use water-based glaze, wood stain, or metallic paint.

GENERAL PAINTING

Use these paints for covering most surfaces, from wood and MDF to metal and plastic. They are all durable and waterproof when dry, although it is advisable to protect acrylic paint with a coat of varnish.

Latex Paint

Use latex paint for covering wooden or MDF surfaces. It is a hard-wearing paint that is waterproof when dry. It is available in many colors, with a choice of matte or satin finish. It may be diluted with water or tinted with powdered pigment.

Oil-Based Paint

Use oil-based paint for covering surfaces that do not accept latex paint, such as metal and plastic. It is a durable paint that produces a gloss finish and is available in a wide range of colors. Oil-based paint is, however, slow-drying and can produce unpleasant fumes.

Spray Paint

Spray paint is useful for covering small areas and for stenciling work. It is a quick-drying paint and has a tough, smooth finish with no brush marks. Apply several light mistings of spray paint rather than one thick coat to avoid runs in the paint.

Acrylic Paint

Use acrylic paint on its own to decorate a surface, or mixed with water-based paint to color it. It is not practical to use acrylic paint for painting large areas. After applying acrylic paint, protect it with varnish.

PAINTING SPECIAL SURFACES

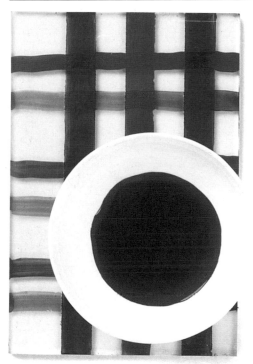

Glass Paint and Outline Relief Paste
Use these products to decorate glass surfaces. Outline relief paint comes in a tube, and should be squeezed to create a thin bead of paint. Then brush glass paint, which is more dilute, between the lines of outline relief paste.

Fabric Paint
Fabric paint can be used on many different types of textiles, but works best on natural materials. After it has been applied, the fabric needs to be ironed or dry-cleaned to set the paint. Always follow the manufacturer's instructions for setting the paint.

Ceramic Paint
Use ceramic paint on tiles or ceramic pots; there is a wide range of colors available. After applying the paint, bake the ceramic surface in an oven to set the paint. This hardens it and prevents it from chipping.

CREATING SPECIAL EFFECTS

Water-Based Glaze
Color water-based glaze with paint or pigment, then apply it over a surface and make patterns in the glaze with rags, brushes, or sponges. Water-based glaze dries very slowly.

Wood Stain
Apply wood stain over a wooden surface to add color without concealing the grain of the wood. It is a dilute wash that dries very rapidly.

Metallic Paint
Use metallic paint for small areas of decoration, such as lining or edging. Metallic paint is a solution of metallic powder and a medium; always shake the bottle before use.

MIXING YOUR OWN COLORS

The easiest way to mix your own colors is to add powdered pigment to white latex paint. Powdered pigment can also be mixed with other media to produce different effects. Mixing it with PVA glue will create colored varnish, while adding it to water-based glaze gives the pigment color even greater translucency.

White latex paint

Raw pigment powder

Pigment mixed with white paint
Pigment paste can be mixed with white latex paint to achieve a range of shades of a color.

PIGMENT WITH WHITE PAINT

1 Mixing pigment with water
Slowly add water to a bowl of pigment and stir with a paintbrush to mix thoroughly.

2 Adding paste to paint
When the pigment is mixed to a paste, add a small amount to white latex paint.

3 Stirring to mix
Using a wooden stick, stir the paint to mix in the color. Add more paste to strengthen the color.

PIGMENT WITH PVA GLUE

PIGMENT WITH GLAZE

Mix pigment paste with PVA glue a little at a time to achieve the exact color you require. Colored PVA glue can be applied over a surface as a varnish to give a tough protective layer that is also slightly translucent.

Water-based glaze is a useful medium for all sorts of paint effects, drying to a translucent finish and retaining brushstrokes. It can also be added to paint to slow the drying time, enabling you to work the paint longer.

GETTING A SMOOTH FINISH

Vertical strokes
Using a household paintbrush, apply paint in regular vertical brushstrokes over the surface. This results in smooth, even coverage.

GETTING A TEXTURED FINISH

Random strokes
Using a household paintbrush, apply the paint thickly, brushing in different directions over the surface. This results in a textured finish.

GETTING A TRANSLUCENT FINISH

Thinning before you paint
To dilute water-based paint to make a wash, mix some paint with an equal amount of water in a jar. Add more water to thin the paint more if desired.

Thinning with a sponge
Undiluted paint can be thinned after it has been applied on a surface. While it is still wet, drag a damp sponge over the surface to absorb some of the wet paint.

PAINTING STRIPES

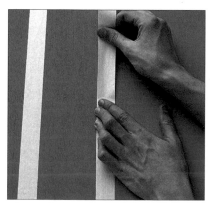

1 Applying masking tape
Cut lengths of masking tape and stick them vertically over the surface to be decorated. The stripes can be spaced evenly or placed more randomly.

2 Painting over the stripes
Apply a coat of paint over the masked area, brushing in the direction of the stripes to prevent any paint being forced under the edges of the tape.

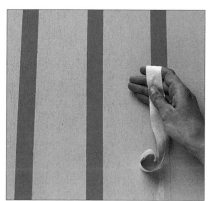

3 Peeling off the tape
When the paint is thoroughly dry, carefully peel off the lengths of masking tape. Clear stripes will be visible where the surface was masked off.

Paint Effects

ANY DECORATIVE PAINT EFFECTS can be achieved using paint, water–based glaze, and a variety of painting tools. Some of the techniques, such as combing, can look very dramatic, while others, such as frottage, have a more subtle effect. You can vary their impact greatly by your choice of paint color. Bright reds and blues will produce a strong result, while pale pink and peach will look more restrained. Although these paint effects may look complicated, they are in fact easy to do, even if you have never painted before. Remember, if you *do* make a mistake, you can simply wipe it off and start again.

STIPPLING

RAGGING

1 Applying the paint
Using a household paintbrush, apply a coat of latex paint mixed with water-based glaze over the surface. Brush the paint in one direction only to produce even brushstrokes.

2 Stippling the paint
Using a stippling brush, gently dab the bristles all over the wet paint. This will produce a finely textured effect. Make sure that you stipple all over the painted surface for an even finish.

Ragging a stippled surface
Bunch up a soft cloth in your hand and dab it over the wet stippled surface. Twist and turn the cloth to absorb the paint. Ragging produces a more subtle effect by removing more paint from the surface.

SPONGING

1 Taking up the paint
Dip a natural sponge in a saucer of water-based paint, being careful not to load the sponge with too much paint. You could use a synthetic sponge, which will create a more even pattern.

2 Dabbing off excess paint
Dab the sponge on a paper towel to remove excess paint. When the sponge is almost dry, dab it lightly on the surface. If there is too much paint on the sponge, the subtle effect is lessened.

3 Applying the paint
Continue to dip the sponge in the saucer of paint as you sponge the entire surface. Let dry, then sponge over the top in a second color to create a subtle contrast.

COLORWASHING

1 **Applying the base color**
Using a household paintbrush, apply a coat of pale-colored latex paint over the surface. Let dry.

2 **Applying glaze**
Using a sponge, apply a coat of darker-colored water-based glaze, scrubbing it patchily over the surface to cover the base coat completely.

3 **Softening the color**
Soften the sponge marks of the colored glaze with a stippling brush. Dab the brush gently all over the colorwashed area to even the tone.

SPATTERING

1 **The basic technique**
Dip a brush in paint. Then, holding the brush over the surface, gently tap it with another brush. Drops of paint will fly off the bristles to spatter the surface.

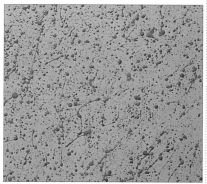

2 **Adding a second color**
This process can be repeated to add a second color of paint drops. Allow each color to dry before spattering another, to prevent colors from running.

LINING

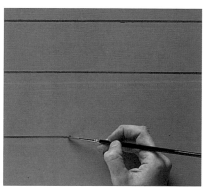

Lining with an artist's brush
Lining is often used to edge items with a contrasting color. Try to paint the line in one movement rather than several attempts.

FROTTAGE

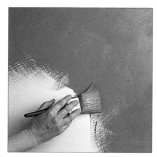

1 **Applying base color**
Using a household paintbrush, apply a base coat of latex paint in random brushstrokes over the surface to be decorated.

2 **Applying a second color**
Allow the base coat to dry, then apply a second color of paint, again brushing it on using random brushstrokes.

3 **Covering with paper**
Lay a sheet of newspaper on top of the wet paint. Don't worry if there are air bubbles between the paper and the paint; these add to the finish.

4 **Removing the paper**
Immediately peel back the paper to reveal the frottage effect. The paper will lift some of the second color to reveal patches of the base coat.

COMBING

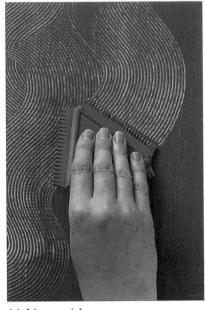

1 **Applying the color**
Using a household paintbrush, apply a coat of water-based paint glaze over the surface to be combed. Brush on the color as evenly as possible, then stipple over the wet paint glaze to soften the color, if desired.

2 **Combing a grid pattern**
Holding the comb with the teeth slanting sideways, pull it horizontally though the glaze to make a combed square. Then place the comb in the glaze above this square; pull it down vertically. Repeat to make a grid pattern.

Making swirly patterns
To make decorative swirly patterns in the paint glaze, hold the comb firmly as before and pull it through the wet glaze, curving it up and down to make even hills and valleys. Comb on top of this pattern for an interesting effect.

CRACKLE GLAZE

1 **Applying the crackle glaze**
Brush a coat of water-based paint over the surface to be decorated. When this paint is dry, apply a layer of crackle glaze evenly over the painted surface. The thicker you apply it, the larger the cracks will be in the paint.

2 **Painting the top coat**
Allow the crackle glaze to dry for at least four hours. Then apply a top coat of paint in a contrasting color. Work quickly, being careful not to go over an area you have just painted more than once, or you will reactivate the glaze.

3 **The cracked effect**
Let paint dry thoroughly. As it dries, the crackle glaze will cause the top coat of paint to crack across the surface, revealing the base color beneath and creating the impression of peeling paint.

DISTRESSING WITH WAX

1 **Rubbing with a candle**
Apply a coat of water-based paint over the surface to be decorated and let dry. Then rub a household candle over the painted surface, rubbing it more over areas where you would like to see more paint rubbed away.

2 **Painting the top coat**
Choose a paint for the top coat that contrasts with the base coat. Brush the top coat of paint evenly over the waxed surface. Do not worry if some patches take a long time to dry. This is because of the waxy layer beneath.

3 **Rubbing with steel wool**
When the paint has dried, rub the surface gently with a pad of medium-grade steel wool. Rub in a circular motion, rubbing harder in some areas than others. The paint will begin to rub off, revealing patches of the base coat.

DISTRESSING WITH SAND

1 **Sprinkling on sand**
Apply a coat of water-based paint over the surface. When dry, coat the surface with shellac sanding sealer (see page 191). While this is still wet, sprinkle sand liberally over the surface. Let dry.

2 **Painting the top coat**
Brush a coat of water-based paint in a contrasting color over the sandy surface. Apply the paint thickly and carefully to avoid dislodging the sprinkled sand. Let dry.

3 **Rubbing with steel wool**
Scrape some of the sand off the surface using a flat-bladed knife. Then rub the surface down with a pad of medium-grade steel wool to remove the rest of the sand. This will reveal patches of the base color.

TRANSFERRING A DESIGN

UNLESS YOU ARE CONFIDENT of your freehand drawing skills, it is useful to be able to transfer designs onto an item or surface you are decorating. Designs can be transferred from books, wrapping paper, cards, wallpaper, and even from fabric. To transfer a design, you can use tracing paper or carbon paper, or if you are transferring a design onto a dark surface, you can make your own transfer paper. Both tracing paper and carbon paper are easily available and are simple to use. They both involve a process of tracing or outlining the design motif with a pencil. Using tracing paper is more laborious, as it involves more stages. Using carbon paper, on the other hand, simply involves penciling over the motif once it is in position on the surface to be decorated. Making your own transfer paper is very easy. All you require is tracing paper and some pale powdered pigment.

Equipment

Very little equipment is needed for transferring a design. The first thing you will need is an actual design motif; look through books and magazines for a selection of bold, clearly outlined designs. The more intricate the design, the more laborious it will be to transfer. You will also need tracing paper or carbon paper, and a sharp, hard pencil to trace over the outlines. Once you have these, all you need is a steady hand.

Carbon paper

Pencil

Tracing paper

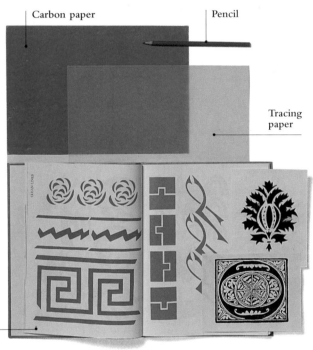

Designs for transferring

Scaling up and down

Draw a grid over the design. Then draw a larger grid on paper; to scale up the design by 100% the squares should be twice as large. Copy the design square by square on the second grid. To scale down a design, copy it square by square onto a grid with smaller squares.

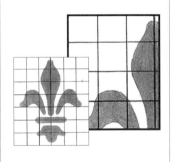

USING CARBON PAPER

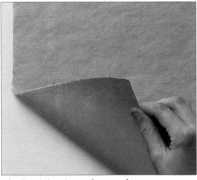

1 Positioning the carbon paper
Place a sheet of carbon paper on the surface to be decorated, ensuring that the inky side is facing downward.

2 Transferring the design
Place the design motif on top of the carbon paper. You may wish to secure it with masking tape. Then trace over the outlines of the motif with a hard pencil.

3 Revealing the design
When you have finished, carefully lift up a corner of the carbon paper to check that you have transferred the whole design. Then remove the carbon paper.

USING TRACING PAPER

1 Tracing the design
Lay a sheet of tracing paper over the design to be transferred and secure it in place with paper clips or masking tape. Then, using a pencil with hard lead, trace over all the outlines of the design.

2 Penciling the reverse
When you have finished tracing the motif, turn the tracing paper over and, using the side rather than the point of the pencil (or using a softer pencil), scribble neatly over all the traced outlines.

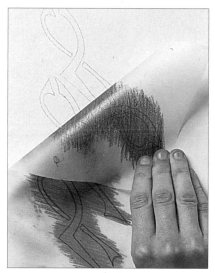

3 Transferring the design
Position the tracing, scribbled side down, over the surface to be decorated. You may want to secure it with masking tape. Then go over all the penciled outlines of the design with the point of the pencil.

4 Revealing the design
When you have finished, carefully lift up a corner of the tracing to check that you have transferred all the design. If not, lay the tracing paper down again and complete the tracing.

MAKING YOUR OWN TRANSFER PAPER

If you want to transfer a design onto a dark-colored surface, neither tracing paper nor carbon paper is satisfactory, because the transferred design will not show up easily. Making your own transfer paper is the answer, as the transferred design will be clearly visible. To make transfer paper, all you need are tracing paper, pale-colored powdered pigment, and a paper towel.

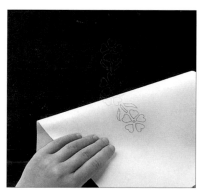

1 Applying pigment
After tracing the design, turn the tracing paper over and dab pigment over the outlines with a paper towel.

2 Revealing the design
Lay the paper pigment side down. Pencil over the outlines. Lift up the paper to reveal the transferred design.

PRINTING

BLOCK PRINTING IS ONE of the easiest and most effective methods of making a repeat pattern to decorate a surface. The basic materials needed to make a printing block are very cheap and readily available, and your designs can be as simple or as complex as you like. Potatoes are excellent for making geometric prints, while cork is more versatile, enabling you to carve more detailed motifs. Printing with sponges adds texture to a design, while using string adds a novel element all its own. Once you have tried these materials, experiment with cardboard, polystyrene, fruit slices, and rubber to create different effects.

Equipment

The items of equipment required for printing are not specialized and will not involve great expense. To make a printing block you will need a wooden block for the base, string, sponge, or a cork tile for the printing surface, and PVA glue to stick them together. Use a marker to mark out the design on the block, a craft knife to carve it from cork or sponge, and a paint roller to apply water-based paint over the surface of the printing block. Alternatively, you can make a block from a potato; use a fruit knife to carve it.

Paint roller

Fruit knife

Marker

Craft knife

Cork tile

Synthetic sponge

String

PVA glue

Water-based paint

Potato

Wooden blocks to form the body of the printing block

MAKING AND USING A POTATO PRINT

1 Carving the design
Using a sharp fruit knife, cut a medium potato in half. Then carve a design in one of the cut halves. The area that is not cut away will be the printing motif.

2 Inking the block
Blot the carved printing block with a paper towel to remove excess moisture. Then, using a paint roller, ink up the potato block thoroughly with a layer of paint.

3 Printing
Press the potato block paint side down on the surface, then lift it up carefully to reveal the print. Repeat the process to print a pattern of motifs across the surface.

4 Adding color
When the initial prints are dry, carve another potato printing block in a slightly different shape and print this in a contrasting color on top.

MAKING AND USING A CORK PRINT

1 Marking out the design
Mark out a design on a cork tile using a marker. This design can be fairly complicated, because the design area is large. Cut out the elements with a craft knife.

2 Making the printing block
Cut a small block of wood slightly larger than the cork design. Glue a handle to the back. Glue the cork design on the block using PVA glue, then let dry before printing.

3 Inking the block
Using a paint roller and latex paint, apply paint over the cork design to ink up the block. Ensure that the paint is applied evenly over the entire surface of the block. Before you begin printing, test the printing block on a piece of spare paper.

4 Printing the design
Press the printing block paint side down over the surface to be decorated, then carefully lift it up to reveal the print. Ink up the printing block again and make another print, lining it up with the first. Repeat to continue the pattern.

MAKING AND USING A STRING PRINT

1 Making a string printing block
Cut a small wooden block. Brush PVA glue over one side of the block. Cut a length of coarse string and arrange it on the glued block in a curving pattern. Let dry.

2 Printing with the string block
Ink up the string printing block by rolling paint gently over the string. Press the string block on the surface to make a print. Repeat to make more prints, inking up the block each time.

MAKING AND USING A SPONGE PRINT

1 Carving the sponge
Draw a simple grid design on a synthetic household sponge with a black marker. Cut out sections of the grid with a craft knife to make a sponge printing block.

2 Making the block
Cut a wooden block slightly larger than the sponge and glue a handle to the back. Paste PVA glue onto the wooden block and stick the sponge to it.

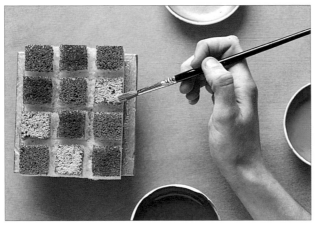

3 Applying color to the sponge
Allow the glue to dry. Then paint a variety of paint colors onto the squares of the sponge grid using an artist's brush for an accurate coverage of paint. Work quickly so that the paint does not have time to dry.

4 Printing with the sponge block
Press the sponge printing block on to the surface to be decorated. Then carefully lift it up to reveal the print. Paint the squares of the sponge grid again to make another print, lining it up with the first print. Continue to print the entire surface.

IDEAS FOR BLOCKS

There are many objects that can be used to make printing blocks to produce a variety of unusual patterns. Here are some ideas using matchsticks, mushrooms, and curtain hooks, but you could also try using apples, oranges, buttons, leaves, and thread spools to print a range of borders, motifs, or all-over designs.

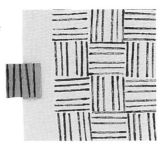

Matchstick block
Cut the heads off several matchsticks, then glue them to cardboard in a grid design.

Mushroom block
Cut mushrooms in half and use them to print a neat repeating pattern.

Curtain hook block
Glue several ordinary plastic curtain hooks to cardboard in an interesting arrangement.

STENCILING

STENCILING IS A VERY effective way of adding pattern, whether repeat or random, to a surface. Although you can buy precut stencils, designing and cutting your own stencil designs is very satisfying. The process may require practice and patience to begin with, but your efforts will be rewarded when you see the finished results.

You can make a stencil from either stencil card or acetate. Oiled stencil card is the traditional material and is cheap and easy to cut, and tough and thick. Acetate makes a good alternative. This is also strong and has the advantage that it is transparent and it will bend around corners. However, it is more slippery than card and can be more difficult for beginners to cut. It is also more expensive. For inspiration for your stencil designs, look through wallpaper or fabric swatches; designs can be traced off paper or fabric and adapted to make a stencil.

Once you have cut your stencil, you can spray, sponge, or stipple paint through it to create the pattern. Always use as little paint as possible; if there is too much paint it can seep under the stencil and ruin the design.

Equipment

Use tracing paper to trace designs, and stencil card or acetate and a marker to make the stencil. Cut out the stencil with a craft knife or a heated stencil cutter; a craft knife is cheaper, but the latter is easier to use. Secure the stencil with masking tape, and apply paint with a sponge or stencil brush.

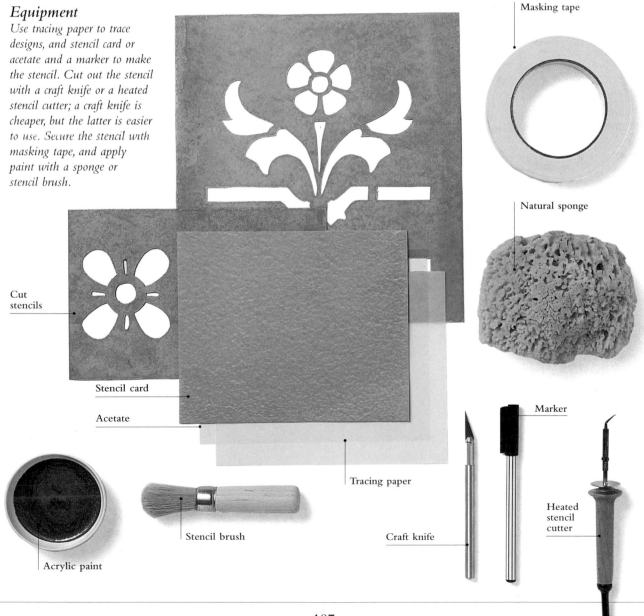

Masking tape

Natural sponge

Cut stencils

Stencil card

Acetate

Marker

Tracing paper

Acrylic paint

Stencil brush

Craft knife

Heated stencil cutter

ACHIEVING DIFFERENT EFFECTS

The most common method of stenciling is to stipple paint through the stencil with a stencil brush. You can, however, achieve a variety of effects using different tools and a range of media. Sponge paint through a stencil for a soft, mottled effect. Use a stencil brush to apply gold powder for a smoother effect. First brush on acrylic gold size. Then, when it is tacky, apply gold powder by brushing it over the size in a circular motion. You can, alternatively, stipple on the powder for a more speckled effect. Use spray paint for a sharper stenciled image with an even coverage of paint. For a more textured, streaky look, rub gilt cream through a stencil with a soft cloth.

Gold paint applied with a sponge

Gold powder applied with a stencil brush

Gold spray paint

Gilt cream applied with a cloth

CUTTING A CARD STENCIL

1 Tracing the design
Find a design to stencil. Place a sheet of tracing paper over the top and secure with masking tape. Trace the outlines of the design with a pencil.

2 Transferring the design
Pencil over the traced lines on the reverse side of the paper. Place the tracing right side up on stencil card, tape in place, and pencil over the lines again.

3 Cutting the stencil
Remove the tracing to reveal the transferred design. Using a craft knife, carefully cut along the penciled lines on a cutting mat to create the stencil.

CUTTING AN ACETATE STENCIL

1 **Drawing the design**
 Sketch a simple flower design on a piece of paper, using a decorated vase or other ornament as reference. Go over the outlines for greater definition.

2 **Transferring the design**
 Place a piece of acetate over the drawing. Holding it securely, trace the outlines of the design onto the acetate using a waterproof felt-tip pen.

3 **Cutting the stencil**
 Place the acetate on a piece of cardboard to protect your work surface. Then, using a heated stencil cutter, cut out the stencil design along all the lines.

STENCILING WITH ACRYLIC PAINT

1 **Applying the base colors**
 Secure an acetate stencil of a flower to a surface with masking tape. Using a sponge, lightly dab yellow paint over the petals and green paint over the stalk and leaves. Remove the stencil; let dry.

2 **Adding color to petals**
 Cut another stencil with slightly smaller petals. Position it over the flower and sponge dark red paint through the stencil to color the center of the petals. Remove the stencil and let dry.

3 **Adding black detailing**
 Cut another stencil showing only leaf and petal veins. Place this over the flower motif and sponge black paint through the stencil. Remove the stencil and allow the paint to dry.

4 **Stenciling flower center**
 Cut a stencil of the flower center. Secure this over the flower motif. Using yellow paint and a paintbrush, stipple paint through the stencil; let dry.

5 **Painting black detailing**
 Cut another stencil of the flower center showing detailing. Place this over the flower and stipple black paint through the stencil. Remove the stencil.

6 **Varnishing**
 When the paint is thoroughly dry, apply a coat of acrylic matte varnish over the stencil to seal the paint and give it a tough protective layer.

FINISHING

VARNISH AND WAX can be applied over either a painted or an unpainted surface, to provide a protective, sealing coat. Varnish is more hard-wearing than wax and is best for surfaces that will be wiped frequently, because it is waterproof and durable. Wax offers less protection against bumps and scratches, but it can be renewed from time to time with another layer, which will enrich a surface considerably.

Varnish is available with either a matte or a glossy finish, while wax gives a surface a soft sheen. Varnish and wax can also be used to add a decorative effect to a surface, by coloring or antiquing it. Use liming wax on open-grained wood to achieve a subtle whitening effect; for an aged look, giving the impression of years of wear, rub dark brown tinted wax over a surface. Antiquing patina has a similar effect to tinted wax, leaving a hint of color, but this finish needs extra protection to seal. Crackle varnish produces the antiqued effect of a crazing of fine cracks across a surface. Use this in conjunction with antiquing patina, shoe polish, or raw umber paint to produce an ancient-looking cracked finish.

PROTECTING AND SEALING

Acrylic Flat Varnish

Apply acrylic flat varnish over painted or unpainted surfaces using a soft-bristled brush to provide a protective layer against scratches. It dries to a completely matte finish and is waterproof and non-yellowing.

Acrylic Gloss Varnish

Apply acrylic gloss varnish over painted or unpainted surfaces using a soft-bristled brush to produce a thin, even layer. It provides a hard, glossy finish that is waterproof and non-yellowing.

Clear Wax

Apply clear wax to painted or unpainted surfaces to give a soft, attractive sheen. Apply it with fine-grade steel wool, then buff it with a soft cloth. It offers some protection to a surface, but not as much as varnish.

PVA Glue

Use PVA glue as a varnish to seal a painted or découpaged surface. PVA glue is very versatile; it can also be used as a glue to stick down paper and cardboard, or mixed with pigment and used as a translucent paint. PVA is widely available and fairly cheap.

PROTECTING AND SEALING BARE WOOD

Sanding Sealer and Superfine White Polish

Use either of these two solutions for sealing bare wood prior to varnishing or painting to prevent the wood from discoloring. Use superfine white polish for polishing and sealing pale-colored woods and delicate surfaces. The main ingredient of both solutions is shellac; superfine white polish is in fact bleached shellac. Apply both solutions with a soft brush; they are both very quick drying.

Superfine white polish   Sanding sealer

COLORING AND AGING

Liming Wax

Rub liming wax with a soft cloth onto open-grained wood, such as oak or ash, to give it a subtle white sheen. Liming wax is a mixture of wax and white pigment.

Tinted Wax

Rub tinted wax over a surface to give it an aged or antiqued look. Apply the wax with steel wool; then, after 10 to 15 minutes, rub it off with a soft cloth, rubbing more in some areas than in others to give the impression of dirt and grime.

Antiquing Patina

This is a 1:8 mixture of artist's oil paint and clear oil glaze. Scrub it onto a surface with a brush, then rub the excess off with a soft cloth to leave a hint of translucent color. Antiquing patina does not dry very hard and requires a protective layer on top.

Crackle Varnish

This is a two-part varnish; when applied, the two parts react against each other to create a fine crackled finish, similar to crackle glaze. Follow the manufacturer's instructions to apply.

APPLYING VARNISH AND WAX

For a flawless varnished surface, apply the varnish with a soft-bristled varnish brush. This ensures that the varnish is applied thinly and evenly, leaving no visible brushstrokes. Apply wax with steel wool, rubbing it into the surface well to ensure maximum absorption, then polish the surface to finish.

Varnish brush

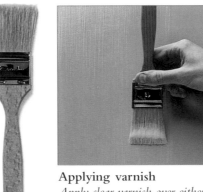

Applying varnish
Apply clear varnish over either a painted or an unpainted surface using a soft-haired varnish brush. Brush it on with smooth brushstrokes for an even finish.

Applying wax
Dip a pad of steel wool in clear wax and rub it over a painted or unpainted surface to give it a soft sheen. Let stand for 15 minutes, then buff with a soft cloth.

USING ANTIQUING PATINA

1 Applying the patina
Using a household paintbrush, apply antiquing patina (a mixture of artist's oil paint and oil glaze) over the surface, moving the brush in a circular motion.

2 Removing excess patina
Rub off the excess patina with a soft cloth, rubbing more in some areas than in others. The surface will now be a slightly darker color, giving the effect of age.

LIMING

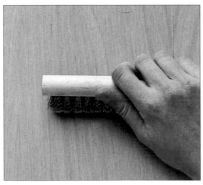

1 Opening the grain
Brush the unpainted wooden surface in the direction of the grain using a hard-bristled brush. Brush firmly to open the grain of the wood.

2 Applying liming wax
Using a pad of medium-grade steel wool, rub liming wax thickly into the surface of the wood, working it well into the opened grain.

3 Buffing the surface
Remove the excess liming wax by rubbing with a soft cloth. Then buff the limed surface to create a soft sheen.

CRACKLE VARNISH

1 Applying the first layer of varnish
Apply a thin, even layer of the oil-based crackle varnish (part one of the two-part crackle varnish) over the surface with a soft brush. This will ensure that the drying time is constant for the whole surface. Allow to dry until slightly tacky.

2 Applying the second layer of varnish
Brush a coat of the water-based varnish (part two of the two-part crackle varnish) over the tacky oil-based varnish to cover it entirely. Let dry for about an hour, by which time small cracks should have appeared in the surface.

3 Applying oil color
To accentuate the fine cracks produced by the crackle varnish, rub a little raw umber oil color over the surface with a soft cloth. Alternatively, you could use shoe polish, which will have the same antiquing effect.

4 Removing the excess
Rub off the excess oil color with a soft cloth. The dark coloring will remain in the cracks, giving the effect of age. Allow the surface to dry.

AGING WITH INK

1 Spattering with ink
To imitate fly specks on a surface, spatter dark-colored ink from a brush over the surface.

2 Blotting the spots
Dab the damp ink spots with a scrunched paper towel. This will absorb some of the ink, leaving softly blurred spots of color.

AGING WITH KEYS

Distressing with keys
Strike a bunch of keys several times against a painted or varnished surface. The resulting pits and scratches will create an impression of age.

SIMPLE GILDING

Almost any surface is enhanced by the addition of gold decoration, whether it is a picture frame decorated with gold stencils, a lamp base burnished with gilt cream, or a trinket box stamped with gold stars. There are several methods of gilding a surface; the technique you choose will depend on the effect you want to achieve.

Gilding with transfer leaf produces a similar effect to gilding with gold leaf (*see page 196*), with the added benefit that it is cheaper to use. It is also easy to apply and is recommended for novice gilders. Metallic powders, gilt cream, and gold paint are other good substitutes for gold leaf and might be preferable for use over a small area. Metallic powders create a dull, burnished effect and are ideal for filling in small motifs; however, they can be messy to use. Gold paint is easy to apply and is useful for fine lining with an artist's brush. Gilt cream produces a softer sheen and is simply applied with a finger or a soft cloth. It can be rubbed over curved or uneven surfaces where it is be tricky to apply transfer leaf.

Equipment

Gilding can be achieved with a variety of media, all of which are available from good artists' suppliers. If you require only a hint of gold in your decoration, you can simply buy some gold paint and a brush, a pot of gilt cream, or some gold powder and acrylic gold size. For more authentic gilding, you need to buy gold Dutch metal leaf, a gilder's mop to apply it, and shellac to seal.

Gold Dutch metal leaf

Artist's brush

Pencil

Gold paint

Shellac

Acrylic gold size

Gilder's mop

Gold powder

Gilt cream

USING GOLD PAINT

Dip an artist's brush in gold paint and then brush a layer over the surface to be decorated. To decorate a large area, use a household paintbrush. Since gold paint is quite runny, it is advisable not to overload the brush or the paint may drip.

USING GILT CREAM

Dip your forefinger into a container of gilt cream and rub it over the surface to be decorated. This produces a soft sheen over the surface. Since gilt cream is quite thick, almost like a paste, it is easier to control than paint.

USING GOLD TRANSFER LEAF

1 Drawing the design
Cut out a simple motif from cardboard. Place the cutout on the surface and draw around the cutout area with a pencil to produce the design.

2 Applying acrylic size
Using an artist's brush, apply a layer of acrylic gold size over the penciled design. Leave until it is tacky.

3 Applying transfer leaf
When the size is almost dry, gently press a sheet of transfer leaf onto it. Press the transfer leaf down with a gilder's mop or soft brush.

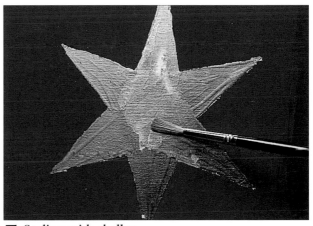

4 Brushing away excess leaf
Carefully peel away the backing paper to reveal the gilded motif beneath. Gently brush away any loose and flaky bits of transfer leaf with a gilder's mop or soft brush.

5 Sealing with shellac
Leave the gilding to dry for a few hours, then brush a coat of shellac over the transfer leaf to seal it and to provide a clear protective layer against bumps and scratches.

USING METALLIC POWDER

1 Shaking on the powder
Apply a coat of acrylic gold size over the surface to be decorated and leave until almost dry. Shake metallic powder gently over the size. Since metallic powder is liable to get everywhere, wear a face mask for protection.

2 Brushing off excess powder
Allow the gold size to dry for several hours. Then, using a large soft brush, gently brush away all loose powder particles to reveal the gilded motif beneath. Any excess powder can be collected and used again.

WATER GILDING

WATER GILDING is a technique that has been practiced for many centuries by highly skilled craftsmen. Although this type of gilding is still undertaken today, it does require a considerable amount of practice to achieve perfect results, and is probably best approached after you have experimented with simpler gilding techniques using metal transfer leaf. Acceptable results are attainable, however, if you follow the step-by-step instructions given here. As the materials and equipment required for water gilding are quite specialized and fairly expensive, it is advisable to start off by gilding something small, such as a box lid or photograph frame, rather than an entire piece of furniture. Even though water gilding is more expensive and more time-consuming than simpler methods of gilding, in the end there is nothing to beat the look of real gold or silver decorating a turned wooden candlestick, a molded plasterwork picture frame, or even a humble paper-covered box file.

Equipment

To prepare the gesso base, you need rabbit-skin glue granules, whiting, and a bain marie. Alternatively, you can buy ready-made gesso. Use silicon carbide paper to smooth the gesso base, and red bole to cover the gesso. For the gilding, you need gold leaf, which requires gentle handling with a gilder's pad, a gilder's knife, and a gilder's tip. Use masking tape to mask off the gilded area, a soft brush to tap the leaf in place, and an agate burnisher to smooth it. Finally, use superfine white polish to seal.

Red bole

Superfine white polish

Masking tape

Silicon carbide paper

Gesso

Rabbit-skin glue granules

Soft paintbrush

Whiting

Agate burnisher

Gilder's tip

Gilder's knife

Gilder's pad

Gold leaf

Bain Marie

A bain marie is a saucepan containing a bowl. Water is heated in the saucepan, which in turn gently heats the contents of the bowl. Do not let the water boil so that it splashes into the bowl – it should simply simmer.

Bowl

Saucepan

196

WATER GILDING

1 Preparing the glue size
Mix 2oz (60g) rabbit-skin glue granules with 4½ cups (1.1 liters) lukewarm water and heat in a bain marie, stirring until the mixture turns to jelly.

2 Making gesso
To make the gesso, sieve whiting gradually into the glue size, stirring and adding more whiting until the mixture is the consistency of thick paint.

3 Applying gesso
Using a household paintbrush, apply the hot gesso over the surface to be gilded, brushing in one direction only to produce a smooth, even layer.

4 Sanding the gesso
When the gesso is dry, rub it with silicon carbide paper. Apply several additional coats of hot gesso in the same way, allowing each coat to dry before sanding and applying the next.

5 Applying red bole
Prepare red bole (fine clay) by mixing it with glue size over a bain marie until the mixture is the thickness of cream. Apply five coats of red bole, sanding between each layer.

6 Preparing the surface
Mask off the area to be gilded with strips of masking tape. Add a few drops of denatured alcohol to a small bowl of water, then add 1 teaspoon of melted glue size. Brush this over the red bole.

7 Applying gold leaf
Cut gold leaf on the gilder's pad with the knife. Using a gilder's tip, lay the gold leaf on the wet surface. Tap it into position with a soft brush.

8 Rubbing with cotton
When the gilding is complete, let it dry for a few hours, then rub the surface with a ball of cotton to smooth it down and remove flaky pieces.

9 Burnishing the gold
Carefully remove the masking tape from around the edges. Burnish the gold leaf with an agate burnisher. Seal the gilding with superfine white polish.

MOSAIC

OSAIC IS THE ART of decorating a surface using small pieces of glass, tile, or stone (which are called *tesserae*). A mosaic is in fact a jigsaw puzzle that you make and design yourself. The design is built up with pieces of mosaic *tesserae,* cut to fit the shape required and glued in position. The finished mosaic is then grouted to secure the *tesserae* and to achieve a smooth finish. Mosaic has a grand history, dating back to Roman times, but its decorative effects are timeless. Today it can be used to decorate tabletops, picture frames, vases, urns, and even cabinet doors. When planning a mosaic, choose a simple design, such as a geometric pattern, to begin with. Then you can progress to more complex figurative designs. You may also wish to experiment with other, more unusual *tesserae* materials for your mosaic, such as broken china, pebbles, seashells, and even flat-backed gemstones.

Mosaic is a craft that allows you to be bold with color, especially when using pieces of lustrous colored glass. You can also develop a sense of rhythm in your designs, as the lines of *tesserae* create movement and flow.

Equipment

Glass or ceramic tiles and tile nippers are obtainable from mosaic suppliers. You can buy tiles either by the sheet in single colors or in mixed bags. You can also use broken dishes or mirror tiles. The remaining essential equipment – PVA glue for attaching mosaic tiles, tile grout, squeegee for applying the grout, and a soft brush for dusting – is available from DIY stores.

Sponge

Broken china

Squeegee

Broken mirror tiles

Tile grout

Soft brush

Pencil

PVA glue

Mosaic tiles

Tile nippers

Goggles

It is advisable to wear eye goggles when cutting tiles and glass, because fragments can fly in all directions and easily cause injury.

MAKING A MOSAIC

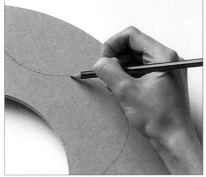

1 Marking the design
Using a pencil, draw the design for your mosaic on a flat surface, such as a piece of stiff cardboard, a tabletop, or, as here, a picture frame.

2 Cutting the glass tesserae
Using tile nippers, cut the glass tesserae into small pieces. Wear safety goggles when using tile nippers to protect your eyes from stray fragments of glass.

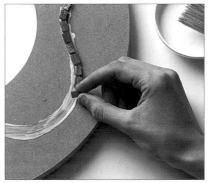

3 Beginning the design
Brush a thin line of PVA glue along the marked pencil line. Lay small pieces of glass tesserae along the glue, butting them up to one another.

4 Building up the design
Build up the mosaic pattern by gluing another line of glass tesserae on each side of the first line. Introduce different shades of colored glass to add depth to the pattern.

5 Adding focal elements
Here, larger tesserae are placed at intervals around the curving lines to add focal elements to the design. The edges of the frame are also given greater definition with dark blue edging.

6 Applying grout
Leave the completed mosaic to dry for a day. Then mix tile grout to mud pie consistency, or use ready-made grout. With a flexible squeegee, apply grout generously over the mosaic.

7 Sponging off the grout
Clean the grout off the frame using a sponge that has been dipped in cold water and wrung out. The grout will remain in the areas between the tesserae, which are known as the interstices. Leave the completed mosaic to dry.

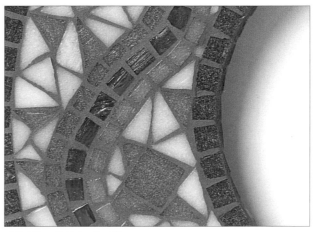

8 The finished effect
The colors of the glass tesserae should be bright and clear. You can achieve this by brushing away all traces of grout dust with a soft brush and polishing the surface with a soft cloth.

USING PAPER

PAPER IS AN ESSENTIAL element of many crafts, and is available in an enormous range of types, colors, and patterns. In addition to using paper for sketching and designing on, you can use it for making papier-mâché, for decorating a collage, and for cutout motifs in découpage.

Newspaper and cartridge paper can be used in papier-mâché. Construction paper comes into its own in collage, where it can be torn and used to create decorative motifs. Tissue paper has a delicacy that can be used to great effect in découpage. Handmade paper and brown paper make good coverings for boxes and folders, and can also be used in collage. Gift wrap, photocopied black-and white-paper motifs, and colorful candy wrappers can all be used in the craft of découpage.

Cartridge Paper and Brown Paper
Use cartridge paper for sketching your design, or for tearing into strips to make papier-mâché. Brown paper is excellent for covering boxes, files, or folders, which you can then decorate with paint. Decorate both papers to make wrapping paper.

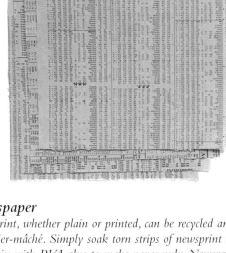

Newspaper
Newsprint, whether plain or printed, can be recycled and used in papier-mâché. Simply soak torn strips of newsprint in water, then mix with PVA glue to make paper pulp. Newsprint can also be used in frottage to create a textured painted surface.

Construction Paper
Construction paper is cheap, highly absorbent, and available in a range of different colors. Use it as a base for collages, or tear it into small pieces and use as decoration. Alternatively, it can be added to papier-mâché.

Tissue Paper
With its delicacy, lightness, and great range of colors, tissue paper is widely used as wrapping paper. Its decorative qualities can be exploited further by using torn tissue in découpage, collage, and even to decorate papier-mâché.

Textured Handmade Paper
Decorative papers can be made with bark, flowers, or even onion skins embedded in them. Tear pieces of handmade paper for use in collage.

Decorative Papers
Use colored marbled or patterned decorative papers in collage or découpage, or simply to cover boxes, frames, or folders.

Candy Wrappers
Colored foil candy wrappers make a shiny alternative to patterned wrapping paper in découpage.

Wrapping Paper
Gift wrapping is an excellent source of motifs for use in découpage. Choose paper with brightly colored bold motifs for easy cutting; alternatively, choose highly intricate patterns for more traditional designs with a handpainted look. Do not use thin wrapping paper because glue may show through it.

Black-and-White Motifs
Photocopy and cut out motifs from books of old prints for use in découpage. These can be colored or antiqued.

DÉCOUPAGE

Equipment

*Découpage needs very little
in the way of equipment, and
much of it you may find
around your home. A sponge,
paintbrush, acrylic varnish, and
PVA glue will not cost much.
Do not compromise on scissors,
however; sharp, small scissors
are essential for crisp neat edges
on the paper cutouts. Blunt
scissors will simply tear the
paper. When choosing decorative
paper, select paper with bold
clear motifs rather than busy
patterns – as bold images will
have more impact.*

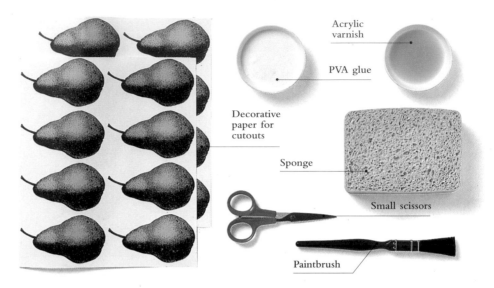

Acrylic
varnish

PVA glue

Decorative
paper for
cutouts

Sponge

Small scissors

Paintbrush

1 Cutting out paper images
*Using a pair of small, sharp scissors, carefully cut out
decorative images from paper. Keep turning the paper toward the
scissors, rather than moving the scissors around the motif.*

2 Gluing paper cutouts in position
*Using a brush, apply a layer of PVA glue over the back of
each paper cutout in turn. Then, after deciding on its position,
stick each cutout on the surface to be decorated.*

3 Wiping with a sponge
*Wipe the surface with a slightly damp sponge to remove
any excess glue that might have seeped out from underneath the
paper cutouts, and also to remove any trapped air bubbles.*

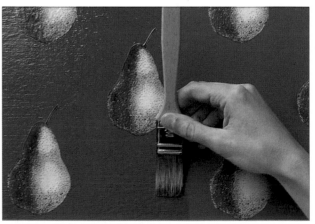

4 Varnishing the découpage
*When the glue is dry, brush a layer of varnish over the
découpage. Allow it to dry, then apply at least five more coats of
varnish, until you cannot feel the edge of the cutouts.*

COLLAGE

Equipment

There are no essential tools or materials required for collage except for PVA glue, a needle, and sewing thread. You can literally use whatever you like or have on hand. Paper and fabric make good starting points for collage, and there is a huge variety available. Try to incorporate different colors and textures into the collage, and choose paper and fabric accordingly. Use buttons, string, and beads for extra decorations; they can be as colorful or as subtle as you desire.

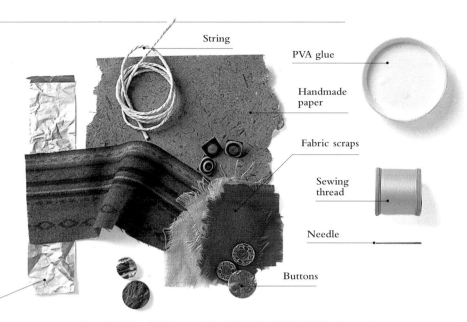

String
PVA glue
Handmade paper
Fabric scraps
Sewing thread
Needle
Buttons
Gold paper

1 Arranging base papers
Sketch a design of simple shapes on paper. Tear handmade paper and colored fabric to fit the shapes, and arrange these on the paper to assess whether the colors and textures work.

2 Gluing in position
Once you are satisfied with your choices of paper and fabric, glue them in position on the base paper of the collage, using a small amount of PVA glue.

3 Building up the design
Glue swirls of coarse string to the collage, and stick small squares of gold paper to the design for extra texture and color. Add painted details to the collage using an artist's brush.

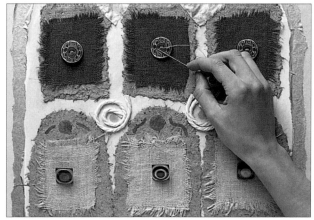

4 Sewing on buttons
Stitch decorative buttons onto the center of each piece of torn fabric on the collage, stitching through all the layers of fabric and paper to secure them in place.

PAPIER-MÂCHÉ

Equipment

Papier-mâché is the ideal craft if you don't have, or don't want to spend, much money. The main ingredient is old newspapers, which, if you save them diligently for a few weeks, will cost you nothing at all. Many of the remaining essential items can be found in most kitchens, including small dishes for molds, plastic wrap for lining molds, a mixing bowl, spoon, and water. You also need petroleum jelly, PVA glue, and a glue brush for pasting paper strips in place.

Old newspapers

PVA glue

Petroleum jelly

Water

Plastic wrap

Mold

Mixing bowl

Tablespoon

Brush for glue

Blender

A blender is essential for liquidizing soaked paper to make pulp. Once you have used it for this purpose, ensure that it is thoroughly cleaned before using it to chop food.

THE PULP METHOD

1 Tearing newspaper
Tear several sheets of newspaper into small pieces about 1in (2.5cm) square. Let the paper soak overnight in a bowl of water.

2 Liquidizing the paper
Taking a handful at a time, liquidize the soaked paper with water in a blender to make the pulp. Strain the paper pulp to remove excess water.

3 Mixing pulp with PVA
Add PVA glue to the paper pulp in the proportion of approximately 2 tablespoons (30g) PVA glue to 2 cups (500g) paper pulp. Mix with your hands.

4 Pressing pulp into a mold
Line a mold with plastic wrap and, using your fingers, press a few handfuls of pulp at a time into the base of the mold.

5 Building up the sides
Build up the sides of the bowl, pressing with a dry cloth to absorb moisture. Then press the pulp with the back of a spoon to smooth it.

6 Removing the paper bowl
Let dry for a few hours. Then lift the paper bowl out of the mold and peel off the plastic wrap. When dry, trim the edges, and decorate as desired.

THE LAYERING METHOD

1 Tearing newspaper
Tear strips of newspaper about 1in (2.5cm) wide and 10in (25cm) long. You will need enough strips to cover the mold with 10 to 15 layers of paper.

2 Preparing the mold
Rub a generous layer of petroleum jelly over the surface of the mold. This will prevent the paper from sticking to the mold while it is drying.

3 Pasting paper to the mold
Using PVA glue diluted with water in the proportion of 3 parts PVA to 1 part water, paste strips of paper over the mold, overlapping them for strength.

4 Building up the layers
Continue pasting layers of paper strips over the mold until it is covered with between 10 and 15 layers in total. Let the whole thing dry for approximately 48 hours in a warm place.

5 Removing from the mold
Ease back the edges of the paper dish, and peel it away from the mold. Clean the underside with a cloth and trim the edges with scissors. Decorate the dish as desired.

THE SEWING BOX

YOU DO NOT NEED much equipment to get started in sewing. A needle, some thread, and a pair of scissors are enough to begin with. But, if you want to be able to sew on more than a button, you will need to stock up your sewing box with a few more basic tools and materials.

Invest in at least two pairs of scissors. Keep a small pair for snipping threads, and a larger pair for cutting out fabric. You will also need some tailor's chalk or a vanishing pen or pencil for marking fabric; use a tape measure for accurate measuring. Keep a range of sewing threads and needles for use with different fabrics; pins are essential for securing fabric layers together. A basic sewing machine will save time when sewing, while an iron is vital for pressing seams and hems as you sew, to produce a neat finish.

MARKING AND CUTTING

For perfect results, you need to take as much care over measuring and marking as actually sewing.

Dressmaker's scissors must be sharp to give a clean cut.

A flexible tape measure is an essential part of the sewing kit.

Mark out fabrics with a vanishing pen, and the marks will disappear after time.

Use small, sharp scissors for snipping threads and trimming seams.

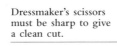

Marks made with tailor's chalk can be brushed off the fabric afterward.

MAKING

Always use the correct needle and thread for the job at hand.

Use pins to secure fabric layers together before stitching.

Sharp needles, in a variety of lengths and thicknesses, are used for hand sewing.

Tapestry needles are for needle-point; they are blunt-ended to avoid splitting the canvas threads.

Use embroidery thread for hand embroidery and quilting, and in collage.

Basting thread is thicker than sewing thread; use it for sewing temporary stitches.

Sewing machine threads can be used for stitching with a machine or by hand.

HOME ELECTRICAL EQUIPMENT

Iron

An iron is essential for pressing a piece of sewing, such as seams and hems, after stitching. This gives a neat finish to a sewn item.

Sewing Machine

There is a huge variety of sewing machines on the market. To begin with, choose a basic one that can stitch straight and zigzag stitch, and go forward and backward.

CHOOSING FABRIC

Calico
Use calico as a backing fabric for cushion covers, or for making simple curtains. It is a plain cotton fabric available bleached (top) or unbleached (bottom).

Muslin
Muslin is ideal for making soft, draped curtains. It is a delicately woven, fine cotton fabric that is available bleached (top) or unbleached (bottom).

Printed Cottons
Use printed cotton for most home-furnishing uses. It is easy to sew, hard-wearing, and washable, and is available in a range of colors, patterns, and weights.

Netting
Use both of these sheer fabrics for appliquéd decoration. Silk organza (top) is a fine, shiny fabric; nylon tulle (bottom) is a transparent net.

Canvas and Burlap
Canvas (top) is a strong woven fabric used in needlepoint. Burlap (bottom) is a strong, coarse, loosely woven fabric used for rug hooking, appliqué, and collage.

Silks
Silk is ideal for use in appliqué and patchwork. It is a fine, soft, lustrous fabric and is available in a huge range of colors and weights.

Upholstery Fabric
Use upholstery fabric for making curtains and seat covers. It is strong and durable, usually made from cotton, and available in a wide choice of colors.

Felt
Felt is especially suitable for appliqué because it does not fray when cut. It is a soft fabric made from wool, and it can be bought in a wide range of colors.

Cords and Braids
These are useful for edging cushions and seat covers to provide a colorful finishing touch. They are available in silky finishes or heavier woolen-type fibers.

BASIC SEWING TECHNIQUES

KNOWING HOW TO SEW is one of those fundamental lessons that once learned will never be forgotten, and will always come in handy, whether you plan to sew your own slipcovers, or simply alter a pair of curtains. Learning the basic techniques of sewing is not difficult, and there are not many of them. Once you have mastered these, you can go on to discover the decorative delights of patchwork, quilting, and appliqué.

Owning, or having access to, a sewing machine is not essential, but it does speed up stitching basic seams and hems, and means that you can run up a cushion cover or hem curtains very quickly. Making a cushion cover is a useful sewing technique, because it enables you to coordinate your upholstery. There are several methods of making cushion covers. Two of the simpler ways are detailed here: the flap cushion cover and the closed cushion cover.

SEWING A SEAM

1 Pinning the fabric
Place two pieces of fabric together, right sides facing and raw edges matching. Pin the two layers together ⅝in (1.5 cm) away from the edge.

2 Basting the seam
Using a needle and contrasting colored thread, stitch along the pinned line with large running stitches. Remove the pins.

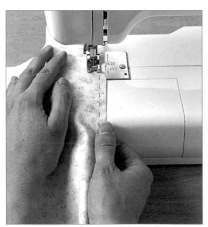

3 Stitching the seam
Using a sewing machine threaded with matching sewing thread, straight stitch along the basted line. Remove the basting stitches.

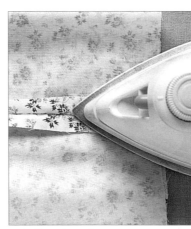

4 Pressing the seam open
Stitch backward and forward at the end of the seam to secure, and trim off the ends of the threads. Then press the seam open using a warm iron.

CORNERS

1 Turning corners
When stitching around a corner, leave the needle in the fabric, lift the footplate, and swivel the fabric. Then replace the footplate and continue.

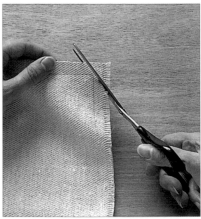

2 Cutting excess fabric
Using a pair of sharp scissors, trim away the corner triangle of fabric (avoiding the stitching) to reduce bulk when the fabric is turned right side out.

MAKING A FLAP CUSHION COVER

1 **Laying out the fabric**
Cut three pieces of fabric, one for the front and two for the back. Lay the back pieces on the front, right sides facing, so the selvages overlap in the center.

2 **Pinning side edges together**
Pin the pieces of the cushion cover together around all four sides, making sure that the raw edges match.

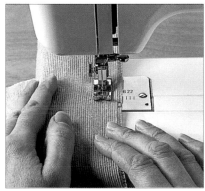

3 **Stitching seams**
Baste, if you wish, and then stitch around the sides of the cushion cover, about ⅝ in (1.5cm) in from the edge, removing the pins as you go.

4 **Inserting cushion pad**
Turn the cushion cover the right way out through the flap, and then insert the cushion pad through the flap.

HEMMING

By hand
Turn the fabric under twice. Stitch the turned edge to the main fabric with tiny stitches, catching only a few threads with each stitch.

By machine
Turn under the raw edge twice, then straight stitch along the turned edge to secure. Machine hemming is visible on the right side.

MAKING A CLOSED CUSHION COVER

1 **Stitching cover pieces**
Place the fabric for the front and back together, right sides facing. Stitch together around three sides, making a ⅝ in (1.5cm) seam. Leave a small gap.

2 **Inserting cushion pad**
Turn the cushion cover right side out through the unstitched opening, then insert a cushion pad in the cover, taking care not to pull at the stitches.

3 **Slipstitching the gap to close**
Using a needle and matching thread, slipstitch the gap by turning under the fabric edges and stitching them together with tiny stitches.

APPLIQUÉ

APPLIQUÉ IS A SIMPLE technique that can be used to decorate both large and small pieces of household linen. You can use it to embellish place mats and tablecloths, throws and quilts, and even curtains.

Appliqué consists simply of applying one piece of fabric over another, larger piece; this is then stitched into place, either by hand or by machine. An appliquéd motif may consist of several layers of fabric, each forming part of the overall design. Simple motifs, such as hearts or flowers, work well, or you can create an appliqué picture using different fabrics for each part of the design. Straight or zigzag stitch can be used to secure motifs successfully, or you could use a variety of embroidery stitches in contrasting colored threads to embellish the appliquéd design and provide a decorative finish.

Take care choosing decorative fabrics for appliqué to ensure washing compatibility with the base fabric. For example, it would be unwise to mix cotton with silk; if washed at too high a temperature, the silk might pucker. Likewise, check that the fabrics are colorfast.

Equipment

Appliqué requires little extra in addition to the basic sewing kit. Use any assorted fabric remnants you may have for appliqué, but be sure that they are compatible. Secure the fabric layers together with fusible webbing, for which you need an iron (see page 206). Use a pencil for marking fusible webbing, dressmaking scissors for cutting out motifs, and small scissors for snipping threads. Use embroidery thread and a needle for hand appliqué, and sewing thread and a sewing machine (see page 206) for machine appliqué.

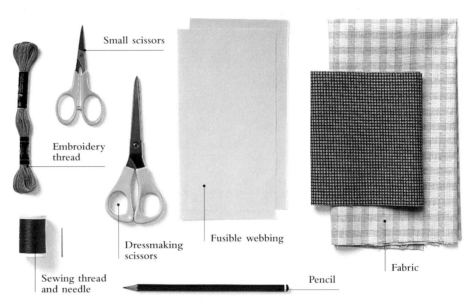

Small scissors

Embroidery thread

Fusible webbing

Dressmaking scissors

Sewing thread and needle

Pencil

Fabric

HAND APPLIQUÉ

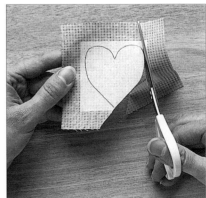

1 Drawing motif on fusible webbing
Using a cardboard template and a pencil, draw the appliqué motif on fusible webbing. Remove the template.

2 Ironing the motif
Place the fusible webbing over the appliqué fabric, sticky side down. Iron over the fusible webbing to heat the glue and bond the paper to the fabric.

3 Cutting out the motif
The fusible webbing will now have stuck to the fabric. Cut out the appliquéd motif with a pair of sharp scissors, following the penciled outline.

4 Peeling off the backing

Carefully peel away the paper backing from the cutout appliqué motif. The fabric will be slightly sticky beneath the fusible webbing.

5 Ironing motifs onto fabric

Repeat the process as many times as you want. Then place the motifs sticky side down on the base fabric and iron in place using a warm iron. The glue will secure the motifs to the base fabric until you stitch them down.

Securing with blanket stitch

Using a colored thread that contrasts with the appliqué fabric and the base fabric, blanket stitch the appliquéd motifs to the base fabric all around the edges of each motif. Try to make small, even stitches to produce a neat effect.

Securing with running stitch

As an alternative to using blanket stitch, secure the appliquéd motif to the base fabric using small, even running stitches in a contrasting color all around the edge of the motif.

MACHINE APPLIQUÉ

1 Zigzag stitching around motif

Once the appliqué motif is in position (see Steps 1–5 Hand Appliqué), use a sewing machine threaded with contrasting colored sewing thread to stitch around the edges in zigzag stitch.

2 Decorating with embroidery

Appliqué another motif in the center of the first one. Then, with the sewing machine set for straight stitch, stitch curving patterns across the appliquéd motifs for added decoration.

PATCHWORK & QUILTING

TRADITIONALLY, patchwork was a method of piecing together scraps of fabric to create new cloth. Quilting was used to secure padding between two layers of fabric to provide warmth. Nowadays, patchwork and quilting are both decorative techniques in their own right, and many styles and patterns have been developed within these sewing crafts. Patchwork can combine a wide variety of fabric colors and patterns to your own design. It can be undertaken by hand or by machine, using any combination of geometric shapes. Quilting can be as simple or as complicated as you please. You can stitch grid lines that crisscross each other, highlight the lines of a pattern within the fabric, or create your own intricate quilting patterns. You can even quilt layers using simple knots.

Equipment

Choose related-color fabrics. For speedy cutting out, a rotary cutter, steel ruler, and cutting mat are essential. Use a patchwork template for accurate cutting of small, intricately shaped patches. Use paper for making templates to ensure patches are equal in size and a vanishing pen for marking out patches. You also need pins, sewing thread, and a needle for hand patchwork, or a sewing machine (see page 206) for machine patchwork. Finally, use an iron (see page 206) to press open all seams.

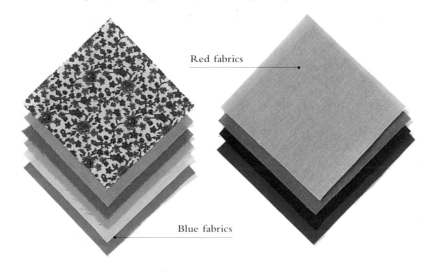

Red fabrics

Blue fabrics

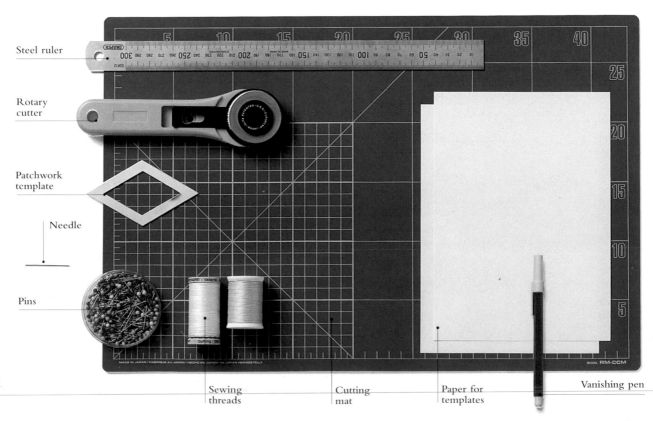

Steel ruler

Rotary cutter

Patchwork template

Needle

Pins

Sewing threads

Cutting mat

Paper for templates

Vanishing pen

MACHINE PATCHWORK

1 Marking fabric and cutting out patches
Using a vanishing pen and steel ruler, mark the fabric into squares. Cut out the square patches using a rotary cutter. Protect your surface with a cutting mat.

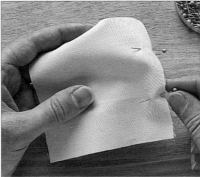

2 Pinning patches together
Place two patches together, right sides facing and raw edges matching, and pin them together down one of the sides, being careful not to allow the fabric pucker at all.

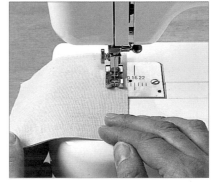

3 Stitching patches together
Using a sewing machine threaded with matching thread, stitch the patches together with straight stitch along the pinned side, leaving a ⅝in (1.5cm) seam allowance.

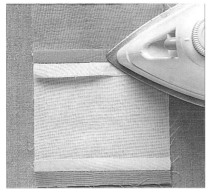

4 Pressing seams open
Stitch more patches together, side by side in the same way, until you have a strip of patches. Press all the seams open on the reverse side of the patched fabric using a warm iron.

5 Pinning strips together
Stitch another strip of patches in the same way, and press open the seams. Place the two strips together, right sides facing and raw edges matching, and pin them together down one long edge.

6 Stitching strips together
Machine stitch the strips together with complementary thread. Continue to piece patches and strips together to build up the size of patched fabric you want. Back with fabric to finish.

HAND PATCHWORK

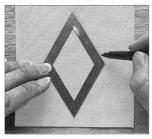

1 Drawing around a template
Place a patchwork template on a piece of fabric and draw around the outer edge with a marker pen. Repeat to draw as many patches as you need.

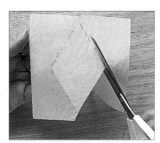

2 Cutting out shapes
Using dressmaking scissors, carefully cut out the patches. Then draw around the inner edge of the template on paper as many times as there are patches. Cut them out.

3 Securing fabric to paper backing
Place a paper shape in the center of each fabric patch. Fold over the excess fabric onto the paper and pin and baste to secure.

4 Stitching patches together
Stitch the patches together with tiny oversewing stitches down each side. When all the patches are stitched, carefully tear away the paper backing.

QUILTING

Equipment

Quilting requires two layers of fabric, which should be compatible in terms of weight and washing requirements. Use either plain fabric or patchwork for the quilt top. Batting is the essential ingredient of quilting; it is available in a variety of weights, giving you a choice of different thicknesses. You also need quilting pins, sewing thread, and a needle for hand quilting, or a sewing machine for machine quilting. Use embroidery thread for quilting with simple knots.

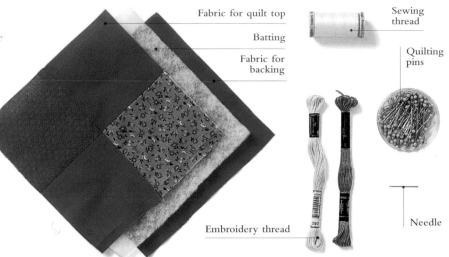

Fabric for quilt top
Batting
Fabric for backing
Sewing thread
Quilting pins
Needle
Embroidery thread

1 Assembling the layers
Lay the layers to be quilted on a flat surface – the backing (wrong side up), then the batting, and finally the fabric (right side up). Smooth them out, making sure that all the layers are flat.

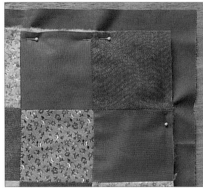

2 Pinning layers together
Working your way around the edges of the quilt, pin the three layers together at frequent intervals. Keep checking that the fabric is lying flat and smooth.

3 Stitching layers together
Fold the backing layer of fabric over the top layer and turn it under. Then slipstitch in place all the way around the edges to encase the layer of batting.

4 Machine quilting along seam lines
Using a sewing machine threaded with sewing thread in a complementary color, stitch lines of quilting along the seam lines of the patched strips. This adds decoration and ensures that the batting will not bunch up inside the two layers of fabric.

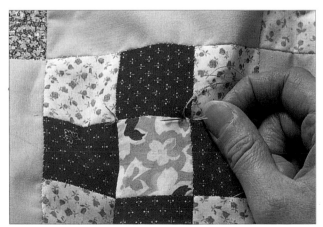

Hand quilting using knots
Knotting is another method of quilting. Thread colored embroidery thread through all the layers of fabric at the corner of a patch. Bring the needle to the front of the quilt, knot the two ends together, and trim. Repeat at the corner of each patch.

NEEDLEPOINT & RUG HOOKING

NEEDLEPOINT AND RUG HOOKING are both techniques that are worked on canvas or burlap. In needlepoint, woolen yarn is used to produce colorful and textured patterns and pictures on canvas, which can then be used to decorate such items as cushions, footstools, and even picture frames. Many different stitches can be used in needlepoint to create a variety of effects; the most commonly used stitches, however, are tent stitch and half cross stitch.

In rug hooking, strips of fabric are used in place of woolen yarn to create colorful designs on burlap. Instead of using a blunt-ended tapestry needle, a rug hook is used. Although rug hooking may appear to be complicated, it is actually quite simple. It involves pulling fabric strips through the canvas with the hook and forming even loops. Both techniques require an eye for color and texture, and a little practice. But, once mastered, they are relaxing and extremely satisfying crafts.

Equipment

For needlepoint you will require canvas, a frame on which to stretch it, woolen yarn, and a tapestry needle. Rug hooking requires the same number of basics – burlap, a frame, a rug hook, and strips of fabric. Frames, needles, and rug hooks can be purchased from craft stores; woolen yarn is available from knitting stores; and fabric strips can be torn from old, unwanted clothing.

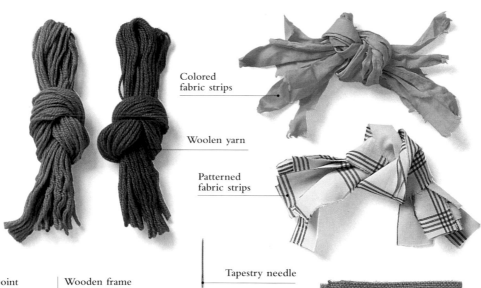

Colored fabric strips

Woolen yarn

Patterned fabric strips

Tapestry needle

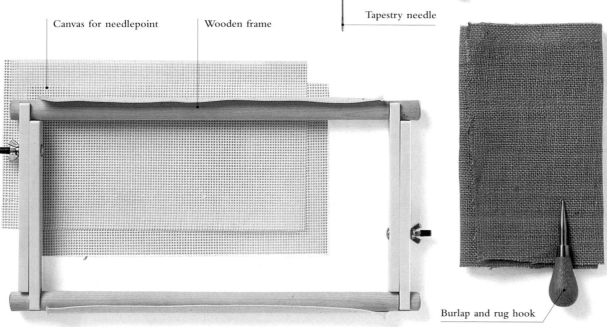

Canvas for needlepoint

Wooden frame

Burlap and rug hook

NEEDLEPOINT

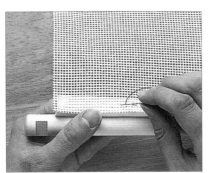

1 Stretching canvas on a frame
Before you begin stitching, stretch your canvas on a frame to keep the work taut while you are stitching. You can either stitch the canvas to the frame or pin it in place with silk pins.

2 Starting to stitch
Take your needle from the top of the canvas to the bottom, leaving a long thread on the top. Stitch over the thread with your first few stitches to secure it, then snip off the end with scissors.

3 Finishing off
To finish off an area of stitching, take the needle and thread to the back of the work and weave the thread in and out of a few stitches to secure. Then trim the end to neaten.

TENT STITCH

1 From the top
Bring needle out at bottom left, take it diagonally over one intersection of canvas, insert it at upper right. Bring it out again in the hole below the starting point. Work from top to bottom, then up again.

2 From the underside
The underside of an area of tent stitching should be covered with long sloping stitches, as each stitch covers two threads of canvas on the reverse side, which makes the piece very durable.

HALF CROSS STITCH

1 From the top
Bring needle out at top right, take it over one intersection of canvas, insert it at bottom left. Bring it out again in the hole next to the starting point. Work from top to bottom and up again.

2 From the underside
Although half cross stitch looks the same as tent stitch from the top, the underside of the canvas will be covered with small horizontal stitches, as each stitch covers only one canvas thread on the reverse.

RUG HOOKING

1 Stretching burlap on a frame
Draw a simple design on burlap using a marker pen. Then stretch the burlap over a frame, securing the sides with drawing pins.

2 Inserting rug hook
Holding a strip of fabric beneath the burlap, insert the tip of the rug hook through a hole in the burlap at the point of the design where you want to start.

3 Hooking fabric
From underneath the burlap, loop the fabric on the rug hook, then carefully pull the rug hook back through the burlap from above to create a loop on the surface.

4 Looping the fabric
Remove the hook, then insert it in the burlap next to the first loop. Pull another loop of fabric through. Build up the design in this way, changing color as required.

STENCILS & TEMPLATES

Stencils for Cabinet Doors

To decorate cabinet doors like the project featured in this book (see page 73), enlarge each of these stencils by 200%, then 108%. Each of these fruit stencils has two parts. Use the first stencil (A) in each case to create the main shape of the fruit. Then position the second stencil (B) over the first and stencil with a paler color to add detailing.

Whole lemon

A

B

Peeling orange, side view

A

Peeling orange

A

B

Slice of lemon

A

B

Slice of lime

A

B

Slice of orange

A

B

Melon slices

A B

A B

A B

Stencils for Headboard

To decorate a single headboard like the one featured in this book (see page 124), enlarge these stencils by 200%, then 120%. You can use all the stencils to create one large design, or choose just a few to stencil corner decorations.

Butterfly stencil

Snail stencil

Bee stencil

Caterpillar stencil

Moth stencil

Tree and bird stencil

Strawberry plant stencil

Flower stencil

218

Stencils for Floorcloth

To decorate a floorcloth like the one featured in this book (see page 154), enlarge these stencils by 200%, then 137%. Alternatively, use the stencils to decorate any other surface you choose. There are three stencils for the braided border: one for the straight edges, one for the corners, and one for the central join on each side. Position them carefully when changing from one stencil to another.

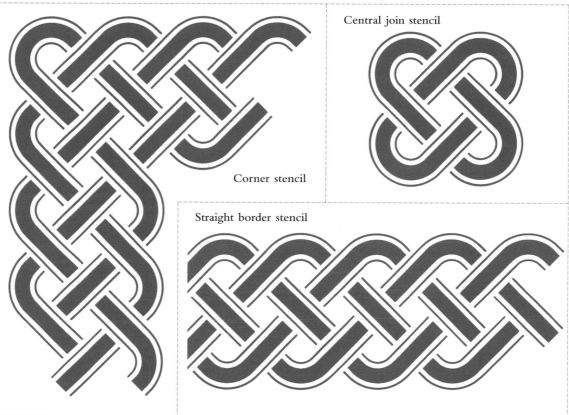

Central join stencil

Corner stencil

Straight border stencil

Tumbling blocks stencil

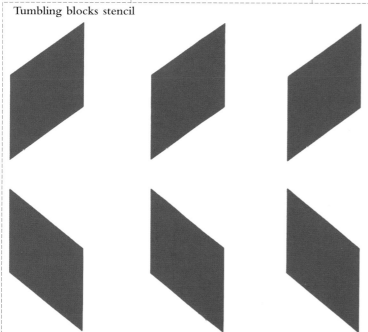

Stenciling the Tumbling Blocks

The sequence of interlocking diamonds works by first stenciling the top row of diamonds, then positioning the second set of diamonds in the spaces between the first diamonds. The bottom row should be stenciled in a contrasting color. Careful alignment is critical to the success of the design.

Needlepoint Cushion Template

Enlarge the template to fit your cushion panel (see page 60) and transfer the design onto the canvas. Stitch the design using a combination of the following DMC embroidery threads:

Greens – 936, 934, 937, 730, 501, 500, 935
Browns – 921, 919, 900, 918, 301, 400
Golds – 833, 831, 783, 781, 782; and Perlé No. 5

Stencils for Hammock

*If you want to decorate a hammock like the one featured
in this book (see page 160), enlarge these stencils by 200%, then
120%. Alternatively, use the stencils at any size to decorate any
surface. Position the shell stencil as illustrated in the diagram below
to create a row of shells.*

Seaweed stencil

Shell stencil

Central shell and dolphins

Hammock borders

MATERIALS DIRECTORY

Many of the general tools, paints, and adhesives in this book are available from DIY or hardware stores. Sewing tools, fabrics, frames, and yarns are available from department stores or craft shops. More specialized equipment may be obtained from the following suppliers:

WOODWORKER'S SUPPLY, INC.
5604 Alameda Place
Albuquerque, NM 87113
Tel: (505) 821-0500
Fax: (505) 821-7331
Woodworking tools and equipment; call for catalog; phone, mail, and fax orders.

THE ARTIST'S CLUB
P.O. Box 8930
Vancouver, WA 98668 8930
Tel: (800) 845-6507
Fax: (360) 260-8877
Craft painting supplies; call for catalog; phone, fax, and mail orders.

PEARL PAINT CO.
308 Canal Street
New York, NY 10013
Tel: (800) 221-6845
Fax: (212) 431-7932 x2297
Art, craft, and graphic discount centers; call for catlog and store locations; mail orders and worldwide shipping.

CIRCLE CRAFT SUPPLIES
P.O. Box 3000
Dover, FL 33527
Tel: (813) 659-0992
Fax: (813) 659-0017
General craft supplies; catalog and mail order service available.

KATE'S PAPERIE
561 Broadway
New York, NY 10012
Tel: (212) 941-9816
Tel: (800) 809-9880
Decorative papers; call for catalog, mail orders, and by-mail swatch selection.

DICK BLICK
P.O. Box 1267
Galesburg, IL 61402
Tel: (800) 447-8192
Silk screens, fabric paints, craft materials; catalog; mail and phone orders.

CLOTILDE, INC.
10086 Sew Smart Way, B8031
Stevens Point, WI 54481-8031
Tel: (800) 772-2891
International Fax: (715) 341-3082
Sewing notions and equipment; mail, phone, and fax orders.

BUFFALO BATT AND FELT CORP.
3307 Walden Ave.
Depew, NY 14043
Tel: (716) 683-8928
Wholesale pillow inserts and fiberfill; brochure available; mail, phone, and fax orders.

CONNECTING THREADS
P.O. Box 8940
Vancouver, WA 98668-8940
Tel: (800) 574-6454
Fax: (360) 260-8877
Discount fabric, batts, and sewing notions; call for catalog; phone, fax, and mail orders.

BOLEK'S CRAFT SUPPLIES, INC.
330 N. Tuscarawas Ave.
P.O. Box 465
Dover, OH 44622-0465
Tel: (800) 743-2723
Fax: (800) 649-3735
General craft supplies; catalog available; mail, phone, and fax orders.

ARTISTS DIRECTORY

THE AUTHOR
pp.22–25, 44–45, 67, 78–81, 148–149, 164–167, 168 (bottom)

TÉRÈSE AUTON
pp.60–63
20 St. Brannocks Road
Manchester, UK
M21 0UP

SALLY BURTON
pp.48–49, 102–105, 140–141
2A Curtis Road
Newcastle upon Tyne, UK
NE4 9BH

MARIA CHAMBERS
pp.54–55
Park Barn Cottage
Corsley, Near Warminster
Wiltshire, UK
BA12 7QH

ALISON COURTENAY-DUNN
pp.111
374a Camden Road
London, UK
N7 0LG

LLOYD FARMAR
pp.138–139, 152–153
24 Wrentham Avenue
London, UK
NW10 3HA

VICTOR STUART GRAHAM
pp.136–137, 142–145
78 Montpelier Road
Brighton
East Sussex, UK
BN1 3BD

ELAINE GREEN
pp.73–75, 124–125, 146–147, 154–157, 160–161, 168 (top)
Ladbrook Cottage
Penn Lane
Tanworth in Arden
West Midlands, UK
B94 5HJ

PENNY GRIST
pp.92–95
4 Hampton Row
Bathwick
Bath, UK
BA2 6QS, UK

KATE HAXELL
pp.106–107, 116–121
25 Torridon House
Randolph Gardens
London, UK
NW6 5HP

JAYNE KEELEY
pp.18–21, 64–66, 72 (bottom right), 82–83, 96–97, 112–113
8 Meadow Road
London, UK
SW19 2ND

ALICE LEACH
pp.26–29
57 Pennard Road
London, UK
W12 8DW

SARAH LUGG
pp.12–13, 98–101, 122–123
24D East Heath Road
London, UK
NW3 1EB

LORNA MOFFAT
pp.32–33, 38–41, 46–47, 56–57, 76–77, 126–129
3 Hobday Cottages
The Lees
Boughton Lees
Ashford
Kent, UK
TN25 4HX

CHRIS MOWE
pp.16–17
Stockingate
Coton Clanford
Staffordshire, UK
ST18 9PB

JANE NEWDICK
pp.86–89, 130–131, 134–135, 158–159, 162–163
Dale House
West Burton
Pulborough
West Sussex
RH20 1HD
Tel: 01798 831236

MAGGIE PHILO
pp.34–35, 42–43, 52–53, 58–59, 70–72, 84–85, 108–110
18 Walpole Road
Kemp Town
Brighton
East Sussex, UK
BN2 2EA

HELEN RAWLINSON
pp.36–37
44A Brighton Road
London, UK
N16 8EG

AMANDA TOWNEND
pp.14–15
150 Barlow Moor Road
West Didsbury
Manchester, UK
M20 2UT

INDEX

ACKNOWLEDGMENTS

This book, more than most, is a result of team effort. It could not possibly have been put together without the unbelievable organizational skills and enviably clear head of Heather Dewhurst. She is the diminutive Titan who shaped the original mass and made it into a book. Clive Streeter took most of the pictures and made the process into a pleasure, using an irresistible mixture of patience, guile, good humor, Amy, Andy, and Arty, great food, and a camera or two. Steve Wooster designed the book with intelligence, awesome talent, and exasperatingly high standards. Colin Ziegler, Claire Graham, and Claire Waite contended heroically with the publishing side of it all. Sam Lloyd and Marnie Searchwell were responsible for entire sections of the book and worked with speed and faultless competence. These were the sections created by Alison Dunn, who has the miraculous ability to make something from nothing. For allowing us to poach Alison, and for the copious materials we used I am indebted to the generosity of my sister, Jocasta, and her store, Paint Magic. And then there were the brilliant people who came up with the projects, the heart and point of the book, for whose efforts and ingenuity no praise suffices. They conformed to the mad complexities of a step-by-step book without demur or disaster, and the result is a collection of mouthwatering and achievable projects and techniques. With gratitude and admiration I would like to thank them all, and in particular a handful of valiant souls who pulled particularly spectacular rabbits out of unpromising hats – Jane Newdick, whose classy projects set this book's tone, Jayne Keeley, who makes everything she touches stylish and beautiful, and my dear multitalented friend, Kate Haxell. To these and everyone else who shared their hard-won expertise to make this an exciting book, thank you.

The following companies kindly loaned props for photography:
Bogod Machine Company
Great Sutton Street, London EC1
Sewing machine on pp. 36, 49, 63, 140, 160

Magpies, 152 Wandsworth Bridge Road, Fulham, London SW6 2UH. Tel: 0171-736 3738
Antiques and bric-à-brac

The paper used to decorate the fishy clock on p.72 was illustrated by Jane Ray for Roger la Borde.